THiNK

STUDENT'S BOOK 4A

Herbert Puchta, Jeff Stranks & Peter Lewis-Jones

CONTENTS

Welcome p 4

A A lucky pilot; Descriptive verbs; Phrasal verbs; Childhood memories; Elements of a story; Talking about past routines

B Future plans; Life plans; Future continuous; Future perfect; Being emphatic: *so* and *such*; Extreme adjectives

C Conversations; Personality; Using *should*; Career paths; Decisions; Permission

D A change of lifestyle?; Reporting verbs; Negative adjectives; Another country; Changes; Regrets: *I wish … / If only …*

	FUNCTIONS & SPEAKING	GRAMMAR	VOCABULARY
Unit 1 **Survival** p 12	Issuing and accepting a challenge Discussing situations and your emotional reactions to them	Verbs followed by infinitive or gerund Verbs which take gerund and infinitive with different meanings: *remember, try, stop, regret, forget*	Verbs of movement Adjectives to describe uncomfortable feelings **Wordwise:** Expressions with *right*
Unit 2 **Going places** p 20	Expressing surprise Discussing nomadic peoples	Relative clauses (review) *which* to refer to a whole clause Omitting relative pronouns Reduced relative clauses	Groups of people Phrasal verbs (1)

Review Units 1 & 2   pages 28–29

Unit 3 **The next generation** p 30	Emphasising Discussing the Tiger mum style of parenting	Quantifiers *so* and *such* (review) *do* and *did* for emphasis	Costumes and uniforms Bringing up children
Unit 4 **Thinking outside the box** p 38	Expressing frustration Guessing game to practise personality adjectives	*be / get used to (doing)* vs. *used to (do)* Adverbs and adverbial phrases	Personality adjectives Common adverbial phrases **Wordwise:** Expressions with *good*

Review Units 3 & 4   pages 46–47

Pronunciation   pages 120   **Get it right!**   pages 122–124

PRONUNCIATION	THINK	SKILLS	
Dipthongs: alternative spellings	**Train to Think:** Thinking rationally **Self-esteem:** How adventurous are you?	Reading Writing Listening	Article: Sacrifice for survival? Article: The ultimate survivor Photostory: The challenge An email about an experience Radio show: *Desperate Measures*
Phrasal verb stress	**Train to Think:** Distinguishing fact from opinion **Values:** Learning from other cultures	Reading Writing Listening	Article: Refugees bring new life to a village Blog: From London to Lyon Culture: Nomadic people An informal email Radio interview about migration in nature
Adding emphasis	**Train to Think:** Changing your opinions **Self-esteem:** Developing independence	Reading Writing Listening	Blog: An embarrassing dad Book blurb and reviews: For and against – Tiger Mums Literature: *About a Boy* by Nick Hornby An essay about bringing up children Radio show about bringing up children in different cultures
Pronouncing words with *gh*	**Train to Think:** Lateral thinking **Values:** Appreciating creative solutions	Reading Writing Listening	Article: Lion lights Web post: A problem on Answers4U Photostory: Writer's block A story ending: *'Thanks, you saved my life!'* Talking heads – being imaginative

WELCOME

A WHAT A STORY!

A lucky pilot

1 🔊 1.02 Complete the conversation with the verbs in the correct tense. Then listen and check.

crash | hit | find | add | end | pull | carry
set | destroy | scream | manage | dive

MIKE So, did you see that story about the plane that ⁰ _crashed_ into the ocean?

ANDY No, I didn't. What happened?

MIKE Well this guy ¹_____ off from Florida in his plane – a small one, only one engine – to go to New Orleans.

ANDY Wow – that's a long way.

MIKE Right, and it's usually too far for a plane like that, but he had ²_____ extra fuel tanks. However, after he had begun his journey he realised he didn't have enough fuel to ³_____ on flying, so he radioed New Orleans and told them that he was in trouble. He told them he had to land the plane in the sea.

ANDY In the sea?

MIKE Yes, there was a fishing boat not far away that was able to pick the pilot up. But here's the incredible thing – and you can see it in a video. The plane had a parachute, but it didn't work and the plane started to ⁴_____ towards the sea! But then almost at the last minute, the parachute pulled the plane horizontal, just before it ⁵_____ the water. The impact almost ⁶_____ the plane.

ANDY And the pilot?

MIKE He was OK. He ⁷_____ to get out of the plane and into a life raft from the fishing boat. Then the people from the fishing boat came and ⁸_____ him out of the raft and took him to the ship. He was OK, so he didn't ⁹_____ up in hospital or anything. Now they're trying to ¹⁰_____ out what went wrong.

ANDY Wow – I'd have been so scared if I'd been in that plane. I'd have ¹¹_____ really loudly!

2 Read again. Answer the questions.
   1 Where was the plane flying to and from?
   2 Why had the pilot added extra fuel tanks?
   3 What did the pilot use to try to land the plane safely in the sea?
   4 How was the pilot rescued?

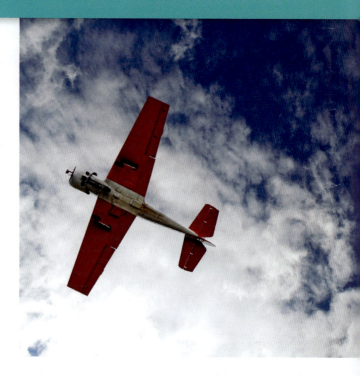

Descriptive verbs

1 Match the verbs with the definitions.

   1 demolish   a to hit very hard and break
   2 dive   b to run away quickly
   3 flee   c to go down quickly
   4 grab   d to destroy completely
   5 rage   e to shout loudly in a high pitch
   6 scream   f to take hold of something quickly
   7 smash   g to hit
   8 strike   h to burn very fiercely

2 Use the correct form of a verb from Exercise 1 to complete each sentence.

   0 The car went out of control and _struck_ a lorry coming in the other direction.
   1 By the time the spy was identified, he _____ the country.
   2 The house was old and unsafe so the local authority _____ it.
   3 Come on, we're late! _____ your coat and let's go!
   4 By the time the fire service got there, the fire _____ for over twenty minutes.
   5 When she got back to her car, she saw that someone _____ the window with a brick.
   6 I _____ but nobody heard me.
   7 She _____ off the bridge and into the river.

4

WELCOME

Phrasal verbs

1 **Complete the sentences from the story. Then read again and check.**

   1 The pilot _____ from California in his plane to go to Hawaii.
   2 The pilot was OK so he didn't _____ in hospital.
   3 Now they're trying to _____ what went wrong with the fuel calculations.

2 **Choose the correct options.**

   1 My father *gave up / ended up* smoking five years ago – he feels so much better now!
   2 If you're bored, why don't you *give up / take up* a hobby?
   3 If there's a problem, tell me and we can *sort it out / blow it out*.
   4 Don't stop! We have to *get on / carry on* running to the finish.
   5 We're off on holiday – I'm *looking forward to / looking into* it.
   6 There are lots of good players here but she's the best – she really *stands out / looks out*.
   7 We had to stay in the town because our car *broke down / blew out*.
   8 All the hotels were full, so we *took up / ended up* sleeping in a hostel.

Childhood memories

1 **SPEAKING** Work with a partner. What do you remember about your first visit to the cinema? (e.g. who you went with, what the film was, etc).

2 Read the extract from an autobiography. Which of the things that you remember are mentioned?

3 Read the extract again and answer the questions.
   1 Who couldn't go to the Children's Matinees?
   2 Who did the writer go with?
   3 Why did they go early?
   4 When did the children usually cheer?
   5 When did they boo?

Elements of a story

1 **Use a word from the list in each space.**
   plot | set | hero | characters
   ending | villain | dialogue

   I read a book last week called *Vienna Trap*. It was a thriller – a kind of detective story. It is ¹_____ in Vienna, Austria. The ²_____ of the story is a woman called Vera, who helps many of the other ³_____ to escape from a terrible situation – they have been kidnapped by a horrible old man called Schwartz, who's the ⁴_____ of the story.
   Anyway, the book's quite good. I thought the overall ⁵_____ was quite exciting and it had a nice unexpected twist at the end. (I won't tell you the ⁶_____, though, in case you read the book yourself.) And I really liked the ⁷_____, too – the conversations between the different characters sound like real people talking to each other. A good read – I'd recommend it.

2 **SPEAKING** In small groups, find an example of each of these from a film or book.
   1 a great hero   3 a great plot
   2 a great villain   4 a great ending

Talking about past routines

Complete the sentences from the extract 'Cinema paradise'. Use *would* or *used to*.

   1 I _____ love going to the cinema when I was a kid.
   2 My brother _____ take me.
   3 The hero always won, and we _____ cheer when he did.
   4 Some kids _____ throw popcorn.

Cinema paradise ★★★★

I'm in my 60s now and used to love going to the cinema when I was a kid. Back in the 1950s, there used to be a thing called Children's Matinee at the cinema in the town where we lived. It was wonderful! Every Saturday morning, the cinema would show films for kids – only kids. They showed cartoons and cowboy films, adventure films, detective films and science fiction – everything that kids loved back then (and I guess they still do!).

My brother used to take me – he was five years older than me. We'd always try to get there early so we could get seats in the front row, or at least, one or two rows back. The cinema sold ice cream and popcorn and we would buy as much as we could, and then sit and watch the films while stuffing ourselves with food.

We loved the cartoons – we laughed a lot; our favourite was always Tom and Jerry and we cheered when we saw the opening pictures. And then there were the adventure films. The plots were often terrible, and the dialogues too, but we really didn't care – after all, we were kids! We used to boo the villains and cheer the heroes. Some kids used to throw popcorn at the screen when the villain came on – the cinema staff sometimes tried to stop us but usually they gave up! The ending was always completely predictable of course – the hero always won, and we'd cheer like crazy when he did!

B AN UNCERTAIN FUTURE

Future plans

1 🔊 1.03 Read the conversation. Put the phrases into the correct places. Then listen and check.

when you leave school
get a good degree
to start a family
and then travel the world
then retire
before I think about settling down

MUM So, Greg, have you thought about which university you want to go to yet?

GREG I told you, Mum – I'm not so sure that I want to go to university.

MUM But if you ¹_____, you'll be guaranteed a secure future. You know, perhaps in ten years' time, you'll be managing a huge company!

GREG But that's just it, Mum – I don't want to manage a big company or a small company either. I don't want to spend forty years doing that, ²_____ and wonder where my life went. That's not the future I want – I think.

MUM Well, so what are you going to do ³_____ then?

GREG I'm not sure yet. Maybe work, save a bit of money ⁴_____ for a few months, you know, get some life experience.

MUM Well, that won't do you much good. In this day and age, employers want people with work experience, not travel experience.

GREG Well, maybe you're right, Mum. But even so, I want some time for myself ⁵_____.

MUM There's nothing wrong with settling down. That's what your father and I did.

GREG I know, Mum and that's fine – it was fine for you and Dad, back in the last century. But the world's different now and people have such different aims, ideas, everything!

MUM Yes, I suppose so. You're right.

GREG But don't worry, Mum. I mean, I'd like ⁶_____ some time. So you'll be playing with your grandchildren one day – I hope.

MUM Well, I'm delighted to hear that, Greg!

2 Mark T (true) or F (false) or DS (doesn't say).

1 Greg and his mum have talked about university before.
2 Greg's father works for a big company.
3 Greg definitely wants to leave school and travel.
4 Greg's mother values work experience.
5 Greg would like to have children.

Life plans

1 Use the words from the list to complete each sentence.

leave | settled | retired | travel | degree
start | career | promoted

1 I intended to _____ the world, but when I got to Greece, I loved it so much that I stayed.
2 I have no idea what to do when I _____ school.
3 She got an excellent _____ from Harvard.
4 He worked really hard and after a few months he got _____.
5 My grandfather worked for the same company for forty-two years, then he _____.
6 A course in marketing is a good way to start a _____ in sales.
7 They bought a house and _____ down in the town where they grew up.
8 They feel they haven't got enough money yet to _____ a family.

2 **SPEAKING** Work in pairs and answer the questions. Then compare your answers in small groups.

1 At what age can people leave school in your country? Do you think this is the right age? Why (not)?
2 At what age can people retire in your country? Is it the same for men and for women? Do you think this is the right age? Why (not)?
3 Is it important in your country to get a degree in order to have a good career? Why (not)?

WELCOME

Future continuous

1 Use the verbs in the list in the correct form to complete the sentences.

study | listen | live | work | travel | wonder

In five years from now,
1 I'll _____ the world.
2 I won't _____ at home anymore.
3 I'll _____ at university.
4 Some of my friends will _____ for companies.
5 I'll _____ to the same kind of music as I do now.
6 I'll still _____ what to do with my life.

2 **SPEAKING** Work with a partner. Which of the statements are true for you? Which statements are true for your partner?

Future perfect

Complete the text with the future perfect form of the verbs in brackets.

Don't worry about Greg. He'll be fine. By the time he's twenty he ¹_____ (leave) school and he ²_____ (save) enough money to travel around the world. By the time he's thirty Greg ³_____ (travel) around the world and ⁴_____ (decide) what he wants to do with his life. And by the time he's forty, Greg ⁵_____ (settle) down and ⁶_____ (start) a family.

Being emphatic: *so* and *such*

1 Complete the sentences from the conversation on page 6.
   1 I'm not _____ sure I want to go to university.
   2 People have _____ different aims, ideas, everything!

2 Make these statements more emphatic. Use *so* or *such*.
   0 Going to university is a fantastic idea.
   Going to university is such a fantastic idea.
   1 The thought of working in the same job for 40 years is terrifying.
   2 Travelling gives you important experience.
   3 It's an awful waste of time to go travelling.
   4 Deciding to settle down is a huge decision.
   5 It's amazing news that you want to start a family.

3 Who do you think said the things in Exercise 2 – Greg or his mum? Write G or M in the boxes.

   0 [M]   2 [ ]   4 [ ]
   1 [ ]   3 [ ]   5 [ ]

4 **SPEAKING** Work with a partner. Which of the statements in Exercise 2 do you (not) agree with? Why (not)?

Extreme adjectives

1 Look at the emphatic statements in Exercise 2 again. Find words which mean:
   1 really scary   _____
   2 really good   _____
   3 really bad   _____
   4 really big   _____

2 Write the words in the correct places.

hot | delighted | interesting | exciting | huge | terrible
scared | miserable | freezing | brilliant | tiny | funny

Gradable adjective	Extreme adjective
1 bad	_____ / awful
2 good	fantastic / wonderful / _____ / amazing
3 _____	fascinating
4 _____	terrified
5 _____	hilarious
6 happy	_____
7 sad	_____
8 _____	thrilling
9 big	_____ / enormous
10 small	_____ / minute
11 cold	_____
12 _____	boiling

3 Complete the mini-dialogues. Use a suitable extreme adjective.

   0 A It's cold in here, isn't it?
     B Yes, it's *freezing*!
   1 A Are you happy they're coming?
     B Yes, I'm _____.
   2 A He tells funny jokes, doesn't he?
     B Yes, they're _____.
   3 A This room's small.
     B Small?! It's _____!
   4 A So, it's good news, right?
     B Yes, it's _____.
   5 A Were you scared?
     B Yes, I was. I was _____!
   6 A Was the film really that bad?
     B Yes, it was. It was _____.

4 **WRITING** With a partner, write three more mini-dialogues using words from Exercise 2 that don't appear in Exercise 3.

7

C HOW PEOPLE BEHAVE

Conversations

1 🔊 1.04 Listen and match the conversations to the pictures. Write 1–3 in the boxes.

A

B

C

2 🔊 1.04 Listen again. Complete the spaces with one word.

1

STEVE   What's the matter with you?

MEGAN   Didn't you see? I held the door open for that elderly lady; I let her go through in front of me.

STEVE   Yes, I saw that. It was very thoughtful of you. Very _____ .

MEGAN   But she just walked past me and didn't say 'thank you'. She didn't even look at me! It's so _____ , I think.

STEVE   Oh, you _____ get so worked up. She was probably just thinking about something else.

2

MILLY   Hi, Jack. Here are your headphones.

JACK   My headphones! I've been looking for them. So, *you* took them?

MILLY   Yes – sorry, I should _____ asked you, I know but …

JACK   Well, give them back. You're not _____ to take my things without asking!

MILLY   OK. I'm sorry. But you don't have to be so _____ , do you?

3

JASON   I'm really fed up. I just heard that Paul, one of my best friends, is going to move to Canada.

SARAH   Oh, that's a shame. But never _____ , you've got other friends, haven't you?

JASON   Yes I know, but I'm going to miss him a lot. He's really fun to _____ out with.

SARAH   Well, you don't _____ to lose touch with him, do you? You can Skype.

JASON   That's right. And perhaps my parents will _____ me go and visit him sometime.

3 **SPEAKING** Work with a partner. What would you have said in these situations if you were:
- Steve?
- Milly?
- Sarah?

Personality

SPEAKING Work in pairs. Choose six of the adjectives. For each one, think of something that someone could say or do to show that quality.

calm | cold | generous | kind | lively
polite | rude | selfish | shy | thoughtful
unfriendly | warm

> *If someone talks to you without smiling or being friendly – well that's cold.*

Using *should*

SPEAKING What could you say in the following situations? Use a form of *should* and a personality adjective.

0   Someone has given you an expensive present.
    You shouldn't have spent so much! That was so generous of you.

1   A friend of yours has said something unkind to a mutual friend.

2   Your friend wants to ask someone to dance but is shy.

3   A child doesn't want to let another child play with a toy.

4   Someone is getting angry because another person was rude.

WELCOME

Career paths

1 Name these jobs.

2 Read the article quickly and find which of the jobs in Exercise 1 it mentions.

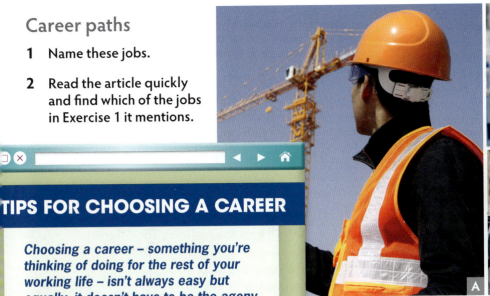

TIPS FOR CHOOSING A CAREER

Choosing a career – something you're thinking of doing for the rest of your working life – isn't always easy but equally, it doesn't have to be the agony that some people make it. Here are our tips to help you make up your mind.

A Don't let other people tell you what to do! There are always people who want you to become a lawyer, or work in banking, or be a teacher. Listen to them, but remember it's your life and it's your decision, so be sure that you're the one who makes that decision!

B Consider what you think you're good at. It's true that things like salary are important, but don't let financial considerations lead you down the wrong path. Follow your heart and your personality – if you're not very outgoing, don't go for a sales job, even if the pay's good. In the same way, if you don't like work that involves paying lots of attention to detail, think long and hard before you decide to do something like applying to study engineering at university.

C Your first decision isn't forever. Some lucky people get it right first time – they choose a job, find they love it and stick at it. But it isn't always like that, so remember – you're allowed to change your mind! Certainly, it's no good agonising for years: maybe you've got three or four possible things you'd like to do, so come to a decision and try one – and if you don't like it, try another one.

D Do something of value. Some people choose their career simply because they think they'll earn huge amounts of money (although the careers which pay the most also have millions of people who never make it to the top). OK, if that's what you want. But generally, people get more satisfaction out of their career if they feel they are doing something valuable for others. It doesn't have to be charity work – it could be a job that helps other people, like being a child-minder. Just don't forget that job satisfaction isn't only about money.

3 **SPEAKING** Put the four tips (A–D) in order to show how useful you think each one is. (1 = most useful, 4 = least useful.) Compare your ideas with a partner.

Decisions

1 Complete the questions. The first letter has been given to you.

1 What do you find it difficult to m _ _ _ decisions about?
2 When do you think it's wrong to change your m _ _ _ _?
3 Can you remember a time when you couldn't m _ _ _ u _ your mind about something?
4 Who do you talk to before you c _ _ _ _ t _ a decision about something?
5 What kind of things do you think l _ _ _ and h _ _ _ about before making a decision?

2 **SPEAKING** Answer the questions in Exercise 1 for you. Make notes. Then discuss your answers in a group.

Permission

1 Use the correct form of *make / let / be allowed to* to complete the sentences.

1 You should never _____ other people make decisions for you.
2 No one can _____ you do a job that you don't want to do.
3 In more and more jobs now, people _____ work from home if they want to.
4 My mother's boss _____ her work late sometimes.
5 When my father worked in a bank, he _____ smoke in his office – can you believe that?
6 This company _____ its employees start work at eight, nine or ten o'clock, as they like.

2 **WRITING** Write sentences about your perfect job or career. Use *make / let / be allowed to* in some of your sentences.

My ideal company lets all the employees play their own music.

D NEW THINGS
A change of lifestyle

1 🔊 1.05 Read and listen to the conversation.
  1 Where are Tom and Ingrid?
  2 Who doesn't want to be there? Why?

2 🔊 1.05 Listen again and complete the conversation.

TOM   You said it opened at eight o'clock.
INGRID And I was wrong! I'm sorry. Don't be so
        ¹_____. It'll be open very soon.
TOM   I already wish I hadn't come.
INGRID Oh come on, Tom. We ²_____,
        didn't we? You said that you were fed up
        with your ³_____ lifestyle.
TOM   True. And then you ⁴_____ me that the
        best thing to do was exercise.
INGRID Right. And I ⁵_____ you to come with
        me to the leisure centre, and you agreed, so
        here we are. We're going to work out a bit
        and then you'll feel great.
TOM   I always feel ⁶_____ wearing sports gear.
        I've got thin legs.
INGRID Oh stop complaining, Tom. There's nothing
        wrong with your legs.
TOM   I asked you what I ⁷_____ wear and you
        said shorts. But I look terrible!
INGRID Look, no one here cares – everyone is
        completely unconcerned about what other
        people look like, they're all too busy doing
        exercise.
TOM   That's completely untrue!
INGRID Tom, I'm beginning to wish I ⁸_____
        invited you. Oh look, it's opening. Come on
        then, let's go in and start.

3 Answer the questions.
  1 Why has Tom agreed to do some exercise?
  2 Why is Tom not happy about wearing shorts?
  3 Why, according to Ingrid, are people not worried about other people's appearance?
  4 Why do you think Ingrid says: 'I'm beginning to wish I hadn't invited you'?

Reporting verbs

1 Rewrite each sentence. Use the verb in brackets.
  0 'Please come to my party, Jim.' (invite)
    She *invited Jim to come to her party.*
  1 'You should watch this film.' (recommend)
    He _____
  2 'No – I won't help you, Molly.' (refuse)
    He _____
  3 'I'm late because there weren't any buses.' (explain)
    She _____
  4 'OK, I'll lend you my jacket, Tony.' (agree)
    He _____
  5 'OK, Alice – I'll go to the cinema with you.' (persuade)
    Alice _____
  6 'Go on – ask him, Sue!' (encourage)
    I _____

2 **SPEAKING** Work in pairs. Tell your partner about:
  1 a time someone persuaded you to do something
  2 a book or film that someone recommended to you
  3 something you would not encourage another person to do
  4 a time when you refused to do something that another person wanted
  5 something you once agreed to do, and then regretted it

Negative adjectives

1 Write the negative form of these adjectives.
  1 happy   _____   4 concerned _____
  2 patient   _____   5 regular   _____
  3 possible _____   6 legal   _____

2 Complete the sentences using the negative form of an adjective in the list.

  expensive | important | logical
  formal | responsible | polite

  0 I don't like spending a lot of money – I like to buy *inexpensive* things.
  1 It's an _____ party. Wear what you want.
  2 The way you dress for school is _____, it's better to focus on your studies than what you wear.
  3 The way he was explaining the maths problem seemed _____. I didn't understand.
  4 My brother never says 'please' or 'thank you', he's so _____.
  5 You've got an exam tomorrow. It's _____ to go to bed late.

WELCOME

Another country

1 Read the blog. Which of the things in the photographs does Hayley not talk about?

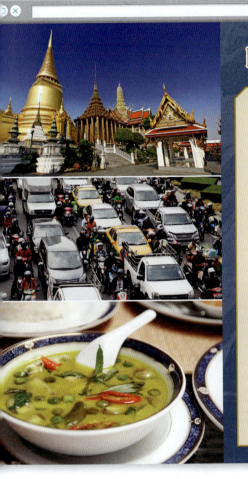

Hayley's blog – from Bangkok!

Hi everyone,

Well, those of you who read my blog regularly know that I've moved – I'm now living in Bangkok, since my parents got jobs here and they're on two-year contracts, so here we are. We got here about a month ago and we've found a place to live, so we're starting to feel a bit more settled.

It's so different here from home. Well, that's unsurprising, of course! For one thing, there's so much traffic all the time, and for a country girl like me, who's used to peace and quiet, it isn't easy to deal with. Well, I guess I'll get used to it, but it might take a while! I just wish someone had told me in advance that it would take me an hour to get from home to school every day – and an hour to get back! But I've made a resolution: I'm going to use my time travelling wisely – to learn to knit, perhaps, but mainly to learn Thai. I think I'm going to struggle because Thai has a different writing system and incredibly difficult pronunciation, but I'm going to put my mind to it and I hope I can make some progress. (It's a good thing lots of signs are in the Latin alphabet too, otherwise I'd be completely lost!) One of my friends told me to try to learn some Thai before coming here – if only I'd listened to him! It'd be quite a bit easier now I guess.

One of the truly wonderful things here is the food – you may remember that I've already raved about how much I love Thai food. My favourite restaurant at home is Thai, so I'm used to all those spices, and I love them. But here – wow, the flavours are out of this world. Well, that's all for now. I'll write more soon!

2 Read again. What three things does Hayley have to get used to?

3 **SPEAKING** Think of two more possible things that Hayley has to get used to. Compare your ideas.

Changes

Use words from the list to complete the sentences.

~~resolution~~ | break | ways | doing well
taking up | struggle | give up | form

0 Hayley's made a _resolution_ to use her travel time well.
1 She's thinking of _____ knitting.
2 She thinks she's going to _____ to learn Thai.
3 She's started learning already, but so far she isn't _____.
4 Moving to another country is a chance to _____ some new habits.
5 I love spicy food, so I could never _____ eating curry.
6 I need to get fit so I'll have to change my _____ a bit.
7 I don't think I'm ever going to _____ my bad habits.

Regrets: I wish … / If only …

1 Complete the sentences from Hayley's blog. Then read again and check.

1 I just wish someone _____ me in advance that it would take me an hour to get from home to school every day.
2 One of my friends told me to try to learn some Thai before coming here – if only _____ to him!

2 Hayley wrote some emails to her friends back home. Complete the things she said. Use verbs from the list to help you.

~~say~~ | wear | find | bring | know

0 I didn't see Jack before I left – I wish _I'd said_ goodbye to him.
1 Electronic things here are really expensive – if only _____ a little more money!
2 I went to a party last night and it was really hot – I wish _____ a dress, not jeans.
3 There are lots of beautiful temples here – if only _____ a bit more about Buddhism before coming here.
4 Our flat here is quite small – I wish my dad _____ a bigger one.

1 SURVIVAL

OBJECTIVES

FUNCTIONS: issuing and accepting a challenge
GRAMMAR: verbs followed by infinitive or gerund; verbs which take gerund and infinitive with different meanings: *remember, try, stop, regret, forget*
VOCABULARY: verbs of movement; adjectives to describe uncomfortable feelings

READING

1 Look at the photos. Can you see *a summit, a rope, a glacier* and *a crevasse*?

2 Imagine spending time in an environment like this. What kinds of things could go wrong? What are the dangers? Make a list.

3 ◀) 1.06 Read and listen to the article to find out what went wrong for two mountain climbers.

4 Read the article again. Seven sentences have been removed from the article. Choose from the sentences A–H the one which fits each gap (1–7). There is one extra sentence.

- A Then something dramatic happened.
- B Simon couldn't talk to him or see him.
- C Several teams had tried before, but they had all failed.
- D Both men knew that it would be almost impossible to survive the situation.
- E Despite his extreme injuries, he had managed to crawl out of the crevasse.
- F And they had run out of fuel for their stove.
- G When he finally arrived at base camp, he was absolutely exhausted.
- H The weather conditions were dreadful.

5 **SPEAKING** Read what Joe Simpson said in an interview about his relationship with Simon Yates after the event. Then discuss the questions.

In a paradoxical way, in cutting the rope, which nearly killed me – and to his mind, he had killed me – he put me in a position to save my own life, and I owe him the world for getting me into that position … I'd like to say I could have done the same thing. I'm not sure, though. So it was never an issue with Simon and I, and we've been close friends for the last […] 20 years.

1 What do you think of the decision that Simon made?
2 What decision do you think you would have made if you'd been in Simon's position?
3 Joe Simpson is now a motivational speaker whose presentations are very popular. Why do you think this is the case and would you go to see one of his talks if you had the chance? Give reasons.

1 SURVIVAL

Sacrifice for survival?

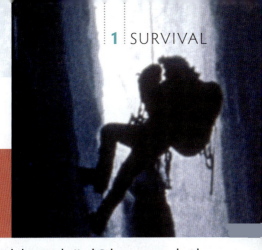

This is the story of two ambitious mountain climbers, Joe Simpson and Simon Yates, whose story was later turned into a film, *Touching the Void*, and it started with an outstanding success. Joe and Simon managed to climb the West Face of Siula Grande in the Peruvian Andes.

1 _____ After reaching the summit, Joe and Simon decided to go back down via the North Ridge, an extremely risky but faster route. Their ascent had already taken much longer than they had intended because of bad weather.

2 _____ So it wasn't possible for them to melt ice and snow for drinking water any more. It was getting dark too, and they knew they needed to descend quickly to the glacier, about 1,000 metres below.

3 _____ Joe slipped and landed awkwardly, breaking his leg. Both Simon and Joe were in shock. They were at a height of 6,000 metres. 4 _____ They were freezing. They had no communication with the base camp, and there was no chance of a rescue helicopter or any other form of outside help. The situation was really dangerous, not just for Joe, but for both of them. As an enormous snowstorm was building up around them, Simon tied two ropes together, tied them around Joe, and started lowering his injured friend. Suddenly, the knot got stuck between two rocks and Joe was left hanging from a cliff, in mid-air over a huge crevasse.

5 _____ He tried desperately for more than an hour to pull his friend up, but without success. The situation was absolutely hopeless. Simon imagined both himself and his friend dying in the snow and ice. He didn't want to leave his friend alone, but the more he thought about it, the more he began to understand that there was no way he could save both his own life and that of his friend.

For a moment, Simon felt like giving up. But then he decided to cut the rope and save his own life. Joe fell away, right down to the bottom of the crevasse. The next day, when Simon continued down the mountain and passed the area where Joe had landed, he saw nothing, and assumed he was dead.

But he wasn't. Joe had survived the fall. 6 _____ For the next three and a half days, he continued to descend the mountain, crawling and hopping on one leg under extremely difficult conditions. He even managed to cross a glacier with no safety equipment or rope assistance whatsoever. 7 _____ The others were thrilled and amazed to see him especially because they had been preparing to leave. Joe's incredible determination and the fact that he hadn't given up under the most desperate conditions had helped him to save his own life.

■ TRAIN TO THiNK

Thinking rationally

Solving a problem requires decision-making. In a difficult situation we may need to make sure that we are not distracted by irrelevant ideas, so we can look at the facts that are relevant for making the right decision.

1 Which of the following facts were relevant for Simon in making his decision to cut the rope?

1. Siula Grande is part of the Andes region of Peru. ☐
2. The two climbers had already reached the summit. ☐
3. Joe had a broken leg. ☐
4. There was no way they could get help from anywhere. ☐
5. Their way back down was via the North Ridge. ☐
6. The rope got stuck and it was completely impossible to pull Joe out of the crevasse. ☐

2 SPEAKING Work in pairs. Discuss how Simon may have felt when he made his decision.

3 SPEAKING Read the situations. For each one, think about what you might want to do and what you should do. Then compare ideas with a partner.

1. You have an important test tomorrow and your friend wants you to go to a party tonight.
2. You haven't been feeling well for several days. A tells you to go to a doctor. B tells you to take some medicine. You like B better than A.
3. You borrowed a friend's bike and had a small accident – there's a scratch on the bike that isn't easy to see.

Pronunciation

Dipthongs: alternative spellings

Go to page 120.

GRAMMAR
Verbs followed by infinitive or gerund

1 Read the sentences from the article on page 13 and choose the correct words – there are two sentences in which both options are possible. Then complete the rule with *a gerund* and *an infinitive*.

1 Joe and Simon managed *to climb / climbing* the West Face of Siula Grande.
2 Simon tied two ropes around Joe, and started *to lower / lowering* his injured friend.
3 Simon imagined both himself and his friend *to die / dying* in the snow and ice.
4 For a moment, Simon Yates felt like *to give / giving* up.
5 But then he decided *to cut / cutting* the rope and save his own life.
6 He continued *to descend / descending* the mountain.

RULE:
We follow the verbs:
- *imagine, feel like, suggest, practise, miss, can't stand, enjoy, detest,* and *don't mind* with ¹_____.
- *manage, want, decide, refuse, hope, promise, ask, learn, expect, afford, offer* and *choose* with ²_____.
- *begin, start* and *continue* with ³_____, or ⁴_____ with no difference in meaning.

2 Use the verbs in the list to complete the sentences. Use the gerund or infinitive.

read | help | climb | be | go
walk | get | buy | show

1 The weather was great on Sunday, but I didn't feel like _____ a mountain.
2 My friend suggested _____ on a bike ride.
3 Nobody asked us _____ our tickets as we entered the cinema.
4 I gave Sarah a copy of Joe Simpson's book *Touching the Void*. She says she's really enjoying _____ it.
5 Can I borrow your umbrella? I can't stand _____ around in the rain.
6 I wanted _____ new skis, but I couldn't afford _____ them.
7 I don't mind _____ my brother with his homework.
8 Can you imagine _____ caught in a snowstorm for hours?

> Workbook page 10

VOCABULARY
Verbs of movement

1 Complete the sentences with the correct verbs in the list. Check in the article on page 13.

crawling | climb | hopping | descend

1 They managed to _____ the West Face of Siula Grande.
2 They knew they needed to _____ quickly to the glacier.
3 For the next three and a half days, he continued to descend the mountain, _____ and _____ on one leg.

2 Match the words with their definitions.

1 climb   3 hop   5 stagger 7 leap   9 rush
2 crawl   4 wander 6 tiptoe   8 swing 10 descend

a ☐ to jump on one foot
b ☐ to walk around without any clear purpose or direction
c ☐ to move easily and without stopping in the air, backwards and forwards or from one side to the other
d ☐ to walk on your toes, especially in order not to make a noise
e ☐ to go or come down
f ☐ to go up, or to go towards the top of something
g ☐ to (cause to) go or do something very quickly
h ☐ to make a large jump from one place to another
i ☐ to move slowly on hands and knees
j ☐ to walk or move with difficulty as if you are going to fall

3 Complete the sentences with the correct forms of the verbs from Exercise 2.

1 They looked down and then slowly started _____ into the steep valley.
2 We spent the morning _____ around the harbour, looking at the boats.
3 At the zoo the monkeys were _____ from the trees.
4 The plane _____ quickly after take off until it reached 10,000 metres.
5 Their daughter was asleep, so they _____ around the house.
6 She was badly injured, but managed _____ next door and ask for help.
7 When I hurt my ankle, I had to _____ around the house on one leg.
8 As soon as I heard Jo was back, I _____ to her mum's house to see her.
9 There was a hole at the bottom of the fence, and we managed _____ through it.
10 He saw the snake and in no time he _____ onto the table.

> Workbook page 12

1 SURVIVAL

LISTENING

1 🔊 1.09 Listen to an extract from the Radio Show *Desperate Measures*. How does the show work?

2 🔊 1.09 Listen again and complete the sentences. Use between one and three words.

1 *Desperate Measures* is a radio show for _____.
2 The winner is the person who gives the most _____ and _____ answer.
3 Dawn argues that it is always rude to speak with _____ in your mouth.
4 Philip argues that it's your own _____ if you get into an awkward situation.
5 He says that if you _____ your room you'll never get into an embarrassing situation.
6 Amanda's imaginary scenario is in a _____ with some friends.
7 She suggests the tactic of looking as if you're _____.
8 She recommends keeping your _____ closed.

GRAMMAR

Verbs which take gerund and infinitive with different meanings: *remember, try, stop, regret, forget*

1 🔊 1.09 Complete the sentences from the listening with the verb in brackets. Use the correct form. Listen and check.

1 Remember _____ a snack with you wherever you go. (take)
  I remember _____ a sandwich during a Maths class once. (eat)
2 I regret _____ it as the teacher saw me and told me off. (do)
  I regret _____ you that you've run out of time. (tell)
3 Try _____ that you don't feel awkward but it won't work. (pretend)
  Try _____ a place where you can sit down and pretend to be asleep. (find)

2 Match the sentences and pictures (A–D). Then complete the rule with *gerund* or *infinitive*.

1 She should stop to rest, but she needs to finish her work today.
2 She should stop resting, but she just doesn't want to go back to work.
3 He forgot to meet Sandra.
4 He'll never forget meeting Sandra for the first time.

RULE: *Remember, forget, regret*

Remember + ¹_____ means *thinking of a past experience you've had*.
Remember + ²_____ means *don't forget to do something*.
Forget + ³_____ means *to no longer think of something that you did*.
Forget + ⁴_____ means *to not think of doing something you should do or should have done*.
Regret + ⁵_____ means *feeling sorry about something you said or did in the past*.
Regret + ⁶_____ means *feeling sorry about something you are going to say or do next / in the future*.

Other verbs

Try + ⁷_____ means *try hard to see if you can do something that is really not easy*.
Try + ⁸_____ means *do it and see what the results are*.
Stop + ⁹_____ means *to not continue doing a certain activity or action*.
Stop + ¹⁰_____ means *make a pause in one activity in order to do a different activity*.

3 Complete each sentence with the verb in brackets in the correct form.

1 On the way to work, Dad stopped _____ some magazines. (buy)
2 I really regret _____ Jim. He's going to tell Martha, I'm sure. (tell)
3 When you go into town, please remember _____ some paper for the printer. (get)
4 Don't forget _____ food for my packed lunch tomorrow, Mum. (buy)
5 Sarah stopped _____ the guitar a few years ago. (play)
6 I just can't solve this puzzle. I've been trying _____ the answer for hours. (find)
7 My ankle hurts. I tried _____ some cream on it, but it hasn't helped. (put)
8 I remember _____ strawberry ice cream when I was very small. (love)

➡ Workbook page 11

 A

 B

 C

 D

VOCABULARY
Adjectives to describe uncomfortable feelings

1 **Read the sentences and choose the correct adjectives.**

   1 When I'm with Mrs Meyer I always feel *awkward / guilty*. It's difficult to find something to talk about with her.
   2 Karen ought to be *desperate / ashamed* of herself – talking to her mother like that!
   3 Carl must have done something wrong, because he's looking so *guilty / puzzled*.
   4 After the earthquake, the people on the island were *desperate / awkward* for help.
   5 We're a bit *stuck / puzzled* as to why we haven't heard from them for weeks.
   6 Without your help we'd be *ashamed / stuck* and wouldn't know what to do next.

2 **Now write the adjectives from Exercise 1 next to their definitions.**

   1 _____ : feeling extremely embarrassed about something you have done
   2 _____ : feeling confused because you do not understand something
   3 _____ : feeling you are in a difficult situation, or unable to change or get away from a situation
   4 _____ : feeling embarrassed or uncomfortable
   5 _____ : feeling worried or unhappy because you have done something wrong
   6 _____ : feeling the need for or wanting something very much

> Workbook page 12

SPEAKING

1 **When you are stuck with a problem, which of these three things apply to you? Add three more of your own.**

   ☐ I go online and look for some advice.
   ☐ I stop thinking about it and listen to some music.
   ☐ I start feeling helpless.

2 **WRITING** Write down three sentences to describe problems and your emotional reactions to them. Use adjectives from Vocabulary, Exercise 1.

   • *I have a test tomorrow and I haven't studied enough. I'm desperate.*
   • *It was my best friend's birthday last Monday and I forgot to give her a present. I'm feeling guilty.*

3 **Work in small groups. Listen to each other's problems and tell each other what to do.**

> *Stop feeling desperate. Maybe the test won't be very difficult. Otherwise remember to start studying earlier the next time round.*

> *Try to relax before the test. Listen to some music, or go for an early morning walk.*

READING

1 **Look at the photos and the headline of the article. Which of these things do you think you could learn from Bear Grylls?**

   ☐ how to build a fire
   ☐ how to use GPS effectively
   ☐ how to build a shelter in the wild
   ☐ how to survive outdoors in bad weather
   ☐ how to set up your own survival website
   ☐ how to tie knots

2 **Read the article and check your answers.**

3 **Answer these questions based on your own opinions. Use evidence from the text to support your ideas.**

   1 What do you think motivates Bear Grylls?
   2 Why are his TV shows so popular?
   3 Do you think Bear Grylls is successful? Why (not)?
   4 What does Bear Grylls think of the way many young people grow up these days?

The ULTIMATE SURVIVOR

When he was 20, he broke his back in three places in a parachuting accident. He climbed Mount Everest at the age of 23. Shortly afterwards, he led a trek across the frozen North Atlantic.

In 2007, he set another world record by flying over Mount Everest in a powered paraglider. This helped to raise one million dollars for the Global Angels Foundation, a charity that supports children in Africa.

His first book, *Facing the Frozen Ocean*, got shortlisted for the UK's 'Sports Book of the Year'. Since then he has written more than 15 books, including the No 1 Bestseller: *Mud, Sweat and Tears*.

His name is Bear Grylls, and he was the host of Discovery Channel's famous TV show, *Man vs Wild*. In the show, he was left stranded in remote locations in order to demonstrate survival techniques. Millions of viewers watched, breathless, as he killed the most poisonous snakes and ate them, climbed extremely dangerous cliffs, parachuted from helicopters and balloons, performed amazing ice climbing stunts, ran through a forest fire, and ate all kinds of insects.

Grylls continues to impress with both his amazing shows, and his incredible charity work. And he has set up his own company, Bear Grylls' Survival Academy, where everyone can learn survival skills from him and his team of highly trained experts.

Recently, Grylls founded Young Survivors – training courses for teenagers, comprising a combination of survival skills and adventure tasks designed to teach the fundamentals of outdoor survival and self-rescue. Those who complete the course are given a Young Survivors Award. Techniques taught include how to build and light a fire, how to navigate in both day and night, building a shelter, extreme weather survival, tracking and hunting and tying knots. A key focus of the course is getting young survivors back in touch with nature and away from technology.

In Grylls' own words: 'The thing I love about the Young Survivor Course is that it is designed to put young adults in just the sort of challenging, character-building and practical situations that help define and distinguish people as adults. So often, youngsters can feel almost over-protected and are stopped from experiencing some of the best things in life – but the Young Survivor Award will challenge and empower them in an incredibly dynamic and fun environment.'

THiNK SELF-ESTEEM

How adventurous are you?

1 **SPEAKING** Write a list of four or five adventurous activities. In pairs, discuss which of the activities from your lists you would like to try (or have tried). Give your reasons.

2 **SPEAKING** Which of the points below are relevant to each of the activities in your list? Discuss.

- [ ] helps you to improve your fitness
- [ ] gets you out of your daily routine
- [ ] teaches you how to assess and deal with risky situations
- [ ] offers opportunities to learn something new
- [ ] offers you a challenge
- [ ] gives you a chance to feel free
- [ ] allows you to have fun with your friends
- [ ] helps you to be more confident
- [ ] teaches you to accept your personal limits

WRITING

An email about an experience

Imagine you are on a Bear Grylls course. Write an email home to your parents. Tell them:

- about the activities you've been doing.
- how you felt while you were doing them.
- what you've learned from them.
- about the people you've met.
- how you feel about the whole experience so far.

Write 150–200 words.

PHOTOSTORY: episode 1

The challenge

1 Look at the photos. The four friends have issued each other a challenge involving their phones. What could it be?

2 🔊 1.10 Now read and listen to the photostory. Check your ideas.

EMMA It's been such a busy week.
LIAM Too right. So many things to do.
NICOLE Same here. And all of these projects for school. It's been fun, though. Hasn't it, Justin?
JUSTIN Sorry?
EMMA Oh, come on, Justin. You're not listening to us at all.
NICOLE Always on your phone doing something or other.
JUSTIN Sorry. I know it's a bad habit, but whenever someone texts me I've just got to reply right away.
NICOLE Seems like we're not important to you any more. You're constantly on the phone. Oh, sorry. Oh, hi, Julia. Yeah … sure I'm going … yes, we're all going … No idea … Hang on a sec. Let me ask … Guys? When's the Chilly Balloons concert? Is it next week?
JUSTIN On the 7th, nine o'clock.
NICOLE Julia? On the 7th at nine o'clock … I'll be at home, I guess. Sure … OK. Well, I have to be off now, but give me a shout over the weekend when you have time. OK, bye! … Right. Where were we?
JUSTIN Seems like we're not important to you any more. You're constantly on the phone.
NICOLE Hang on – it was Julia and it was important. I was only helping her.
EMMA Did you hear that the cheapest tickets to the concert are £42?
LIAM What? That can't be right. Let me check. Here we are. Chilly Balloons … Saturday 7th … tickets from £25.00 to £100.00.
EMMA Oh, that doesn't sound too bad. Thanks, Liam.
NICOLE You know what? We're telling Justin off for being on his phone too much, but we're all just as bad.
JUSTIN Ha! True! Hey, I challenge us all *not* to use our phones for the whole weekend. Not once. I bet you can't.
NICOLE Ridiculous. Of course we can. Why wouldn't we be able to?
EMMA Oh, come on. Three days without a phone? No problem!
JUSTIN OK. Let's try it, shall we? You'll never survive the weekend without your phones. You'll see. Anyone who uses their phone has to treat the others to coffee or whatever they want at the café. OK?
EMMA OK. I'm in.
JUSTIN No phones, right up to Monday morning, starting now. Deal?
OTHERS Deal!

1 Survival

DEVELOPING SPEAKING

3 Work in pairs. Discuss what happens next in the story. Write down your ideas.

We think that two of them succeed and two of them don't.

4 ▶ EP1 Watch to find out how the story continues.

5 Answer the questions.
 1 Why does Nicole's dad think she doesn't answer her phone?
 2 What did Emma do that meant she lost the challenge?
 3 What did Liam do or not do about the challenge?
 4 How long did Justin manage to not use his phone for?
 5 What did Nicole do that meant she didn't win the challenge?

PHRASES FOR FLUENCY

1 Find these expressions in the story. Who says them? How do you say them in your language?
 1 Same here.
 2 something or other
 3 Give me a shout
 4 Where (were we)?
 5 You know what?
 6 (It's a) deal!

2 Use the expressions in Exercise 1 to complete the dialogues.
 1 A I was really busy over the weekend. No time to relax! I always had _____ to do.
   B _____! I didn't stop for a moment.
 2 A Listen, if you find the homework difficult, _____ and I can try to help you. Then maybe you can make us a snack later.
   B _____! Thanks a lot, Georgia.
 3 A This exercise is exhausting.
   B You're right. _____? We should have a break.
 4 A So, I think we should do that.
   B Hang on, let me answer this phone call. ... Sorry about that. Right, _____?

WordWise
Expressions with *right*

1 Look at these sentences from the unit so far. Complete them with phrases from the list.

right? | right away | Too right
right up to | All right! | Right ...

 1 I just feel like I've got to reply _____.
 2 A It's been such a busy week.
   B _____. So many things to do.
 3 No mobiles, _____ Monday morning. Deal?
 4 You know my friends Emma, Justin and Liam, _____
 5 OK, bye! _____, where were we?
 6 A I told you. No technology all weekend.
   B _____

2 Complete the sentences with a phrase using *right*.
 1 You're the new girl at school, _____?
 2 The party was great. I stayed _____ the end.
 3 There's a problem at home. I need to leave _____.
 4 _____, everyone. I want you all to listen ...
 5 A That film was terrible.
   B _____. I hated it as well.
 6 A Can you give me a hand with my homework?
   B _____. I'll be with you in a minute.

→ Workbook page 12

FUNCTIONS
Issuing and accepting a challenge

1 Read the phrases. Which ones are used to issue a challenge? Which ones are used to accept or turn down a challenge?
 1 I bet you can't ...
 2 I think you're (probably) right.
 3 I bet (you) I can ...
 4 That's too easy.
 5 I challenge you to ...
 6 No problem.
 7 You'll never manage to ...
 8 Of course I can.

2 **WRITING** Work in pairs. Write short dialogues between two people, where one challenges the other. Use these ideas and one of your own.

 • eat a doughnut without licking your lips
 • stay awake for twenty-four hours
 • walk twenty kilometres in four hours
 • finish this exercise before me
 • speak only in English during break times and lunchtimes for a whole week

2 GOING PLACES

OBJECTIVES

FUNCTIONS: expressing surprise
GRAMMAR: relative clauses (review); *which* to refer to a whole clause; omitting relative pronouns; reduced relative clauses
VOCABULARY: groups of people; phrasal verbs (1)

READING

1 Imagine you are going to live in another country. What things do you have to get used to? Add two more things to this list. Then put the six things in order of difficulty for you (1 = most difficult).

   the climate ☐   the language ☐
   the food ☐   _____ ☐
   local customs ☐   _____ ☐

2 **SPEAKING** Compare your ideas with other students.

3 **SPEAKING** Work in pairs or small groups. Look at the photos and these phrases from the article. Discuss what you think the article is about.

   - a shortage of jobs
   - the creation of workshops
   - began to welcome refugees
   - the renovation of houses

4 🔊 1.11 Read and listen to the article and check your ideas.

5 All of these statements are incorrect. Read the article again and find the lines which show they are incorrect. Then correct the sentences.

   1 Many people in the 1990s left Riace because they didn't like it any more.
   2 The refugees didn't have to do anything to get food and accommodation.
   3 The refugees already spoke Italian.
   4 New houses were built for the refugees.
   5 About a hundred immigrants live in Riace now.
   6 More local people are leaving Riace.
   7 Many politicians have criticised Lucano's ideas.
   8 Lucano won the 2010 'World Mayor' award.

6 **SPEAKING** Work with a partner and discuss the following questions.

   1 What two questions would you like to ask:
      a a resident born in Riace?
      b an immigrant living and working in Riace?
   2 Do you think things will continue to go well in Riace in the future? Why (not)?

2 GOING PLACES

Refugees Bring New Life to a Village

Riace is a small village in Calabria, which is a very pretty region of Italy, but also quite a poor one. Riace once had a population of 3,000, but in the 1990s a shortage of jobs meant that many of the inhabitants, especially young people, left the village to find work in other places. The only school closed. There were no restaurants and very few shops. Many houses were empty. Riace was becoming a ghost town. But these days it's a different story, because of one man whose dreams have turned Riace into a village with a future.

One day in 1998, Domenico Lucano, a teacher from Riace, was driving near the sea when he saw a large group of people on the beach. They were refugees who had arrived by boat to escape problems in their countries. Lucano had an idea of how to help these people and how they, in turn, might possibly help him save his village. He decided to welcome them into the village and to give them food and accommodation in return for work. The refugees also had to learn Italian.

It was the beginning of a plan. Lucano created an organisation called Città Futura, or City of the Future. The idea was simple: Riace desperately needed more inhabitants and there were plenty of people in the world looking for a home. The village began to welcome refugees from Somalia, Afghanistan, Iraq, Lebanon and other places. Lucano used buildings which had been empty for years to house the new arrivals, and he created workshops for them to work in.

Riace is now home to between two and three hundred immigrants, who live happily alongside the locals. Most of the women make handicrafts to sell in local shops, while the men renovate empty houses to rent to tourists. But it is not only the refugees who have gained from Lucano's plans: Città Futura also has 13 local employees, which makes it the biggest employer in the village. And because of the arrival of more children, the school is open again. Lucano, who became mayor of Riace in 2004, has managed to create jobs and to stop the villagers moving away, while at the same time helping some of the poorest and most desperate people in the world.

Many politicians have visited Riace hoping that they can use Lucano's ideas in their own towns and cities. The German film director Wim Wenders also went there and was inspired to make a short documentary about the village called *Il Volo* (*The Flight*). Lucano himself was voted third in the 2010 'World Mayor' competition, and was praised for his courage and compassion.

■ TRAIN TO THINK

Distinguishing fact from opinion

People often have disagreements because they confuse opinions with facts. A fact is something true for which there is usually proof. An opinion is a thought or belief and may not be true. When you want to know if what someone is saying is really true, it's important to ask the right questions to help you separate opinions from facts.

1. Read the two statements (A). What is the purpose of the question (B) that follows each of them?

    1. **A** *Teenagers never want to travel anywhere with their parents.*
       B *Does that mean that there has never been a young person who liked travelling with their parents?*
    2. **A** *I'm convinced listening to music keeps you healthy.*
       B *What evidence is there that proves you are right?*

2. Here are things people said to Domenico Lucano when he was about to start his project. Work in pairs and find good questions that he could ask to separate opinions from facts.

    1. *All the young people are moving away. Our town has no future.*
    2. *I'm sure these refugees are trouble makers.*
    3. *Don't invite these people to our village. They're poor and will only create problems.*
    4. *It's a bad idea to put people from different countries together. They might not get on.*
    5. *These people can't survive in our village. There's just no work for them.*

21

GRAMMAR
Relative clauses (review)

1 Read the sentences from the article about Riace. Look at the underlined parts. Then complete the rule by writing A, B, C or D.

A Riace is in Calabria, <u>which is a very pretty region of Italy</u>.
B Lucano used buildings <u>which had been empty for years</u> to house the new arrivals.
C They were refugees <u>who had arrived by boat</u>.
D Lucano, <u>who became mayor of Riace in 2004</u>, has managed to create jobs.

> **RULE:** We use a defining relative clause to identify an object (*which / that*), a person (*who / that*), a place (*where*) or a possession (*whose*). Without this information, it's hard to know who or what we're talking about. (e.g. Sentences ¹____ and ²____)
>
> We use a non-defining relative clause to add extra information. We don't need this information to understand the sentence. We put commas around it. (e.g. Sentences ³____ and ⁴____)

2 **SPEAKING** Complete each sentence with *who*, *which* or *that*. Are they defining or non-defining relative clauses? Then discuss the statements with a partner.

1 I don't understand people _____ decide to go and live in another country.
2 Sometimes people don't like strangers _____ come and live in their town.
3 A stranger is just someone _____ isn't your friend yet.
4 Sometimes it's just a person's appearance _____ makes us like them or not.

3 Join the sentences to make one sentence by including a non-defining relative clause. Put commas in the correct places.

0 The people were tired. They had come a long way.
The people, who had come a long way, were tired.
1 The locals gave them food. The locals were kind.
2 Rome is an exciting place. It is my favourite city.
3 I've been reading a book by William Boyd. Boyd is one of my favourite writers.
4 My neighbour Rubens has been living here for ten years. Rubens is from Guatemala.

which to refer to a whole clause

4 Read the two sentences from the article. What does *which* refer to in each sentence?

1 Riace is a small village in Calabria, **which** is a very pretty region of Italy.
2 *Città Futura* has 13 local employees, **which** makes it the biggest employer in the village.

5 What does *this* refer to in each of the second sentences below? Rewrite the pairs of sentences as one sentence.

0 A lot of tourists visit. This is good for the town.
A lot of tourists visit, which is good for the town.
1 Some people go and live in another country. This is not always easy.
2 You have to learn new customs. This can be challenging.
3 Some people are nervous about strangers. This makes life difficult for new arrivals.
4 Sometimes there are differences in culture. This often results in misunderstandings.

> Workbook page 18

VOCABULARY
Groups of people

Complete each sentence with a word from the list.

the audience | motorists | pedestrians
residents | the crew | the staff | employees
employers | immigrants | politicians
refugees | inhabitants

0 People who watch a play / film / concert are *the audience*.
1 People who walk on a street are called _____.
2 A group of people who work for an organisation are _____.
3 People who drive cars are called _____.
4 A group of people who work on a plane or ship are _____.
5 _____ are people or animals that live in a specific place.
6 People who are paid to work for other people are called _____.
7 People who work in politics are called _____.
8 _____ are people who leave their own country because it's too difficult or dangerous to live there.
9 _____ pay others to work for them.
10 People who live in a certain place are the _____.
11 _____ are people who come to a different country to live there permanently.

> Workbook page 20

2 GOING PLACES

LISTENING
Migration in nature

wildebeest A

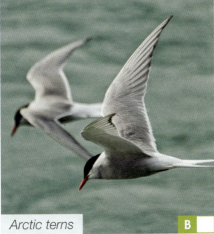
Arctic terns B

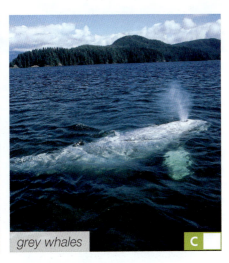
grey whales C

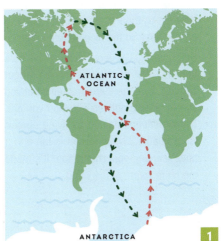
1

2

3

1 **SPEAKING** Look at the photos and the maps. Which animals in the photographs make which journeys in the maps? Discuss your ideas.

2 🔊 1.12 Listen to a radio interview. Check your ideas. Write 1, 2 and 3 in the boxes.

3 🔊 1.12 What do these numbers refer to? Listen again and check.

| 1 | 18,000 | 3 | 2,000 | 5 | 70,000 |
| 2 | more than a million | 4 | 250,000 | 6 | 2,000,000 |

4 🔊 1.12 Correct these sentences. Listen again to check.
1 Grey whales swim to Alaska to have their babies there.
2 Grey whales can be found near Alaska in the winter.
3 The Mara River is at the beginning of the wildebeests' journey.
4 The Mara River is full of hippos.
5 Arctic terns do their journey only once in their lifetime.
6 People know how the terns always arrive at the same place.

5 **SPEAKING** Work in small groups. Answer these questions.
1 Which of the animal facts you heard do you think is the most interesting?
2 Do you know about any other animals or birds who undertake amazing journeys?

FUNCTIONS
Expressing surprise

1 🔊 1.12 Listen again to the radio interview. What phrases are used to express surprise? Can you think of any other phrases?

1 _____ (distance)!
2 _____ ! Good heavens.
3 It's _____ , isn't it?
4 Wow. That's _____ .
5 That's _____ .

2 Work in AB pairs. A thinks of something surprising that he/she knows. (You can invent something if you want!) A gives the information to B. B uses one of the expressions in Exercise 1 to reply, and asks a follow-up question. Then A and B change roles.

Becca's Blog: From London to Lyon

Five not-so-good things about living abroad

Regular readers of my blog already know that I'm a student living and studying in France for a year. Overall it's turning out to be a great experience. But today I've decided to write about some of the challenges that living abroad can bring. Here we go.

A It isn't a holiday

You know those Hollywood films where the foreigner is living a nice, easy, comfortable life in another country? Well, forget it – that's not how it is. You have to do all kinds of things like open a bank account, find somewhere to live, pay bills, and so on. These things aren't easy and they take time.

B Language problems

Before I came, I thought my French was pretty good. But being here isn't like French at school was. People talk to me like they talk to each other – fast! There's new vocabulary which you have to pick up – the first time I went to a hairdresser, I didn't know what to say! Speaking French all day wears me out. Often, at night, I'll watch anything on TV in English! Anything!

C You might not like it

It's possible that after all the excitement of moving to another country, you become one of those foreigners who is unhappy abroad. I ran into some people who couldn't wait to leave France after just a few weeks. Well, there's no country in the world that suits everybody, right? It's always a risk.

D Homesickness

After a few weeks you'll start to miss all kinds of things (and people) from back home. That special food, that TV programme, the friends who you used to hang out with. Well, it's a phase you have to go through. If you're really homesick, go home. Otherwise, keep going, the homesickness won't last forever.

E Not everyone is happy that you're there

Mostly people are kind to me and happy to see me. But there are exceptions. Sometimes I go somewhere and someone says something like: 'Oh, no, another English person!' It's not nice to hear, but you have to put up with it. I find it's best to try and ignore that stuff and concentrate on the nice people I meet.

Still, overall, I'm very happy to be here and I have no regrets at all about coming. Sure there are problems but you can run into problems wherever you are. The experience gained by living abroad is invaluable. Living abroad is fun and a huge learning opportunity too. It's made me more aware of the world.

READING

1 Look at the photo and the title of the blog, and make notes on the following.
1. Where do you think the woman is?
2. Where do you think she's from?
3. What is this blog entry about?

2 Read the blog and check your ideas.

3 Read the blog again and answer the questions.
1. What is Becca doing in France?
2. Why does she say that it 'isn't a holiday'?
3. Why is she sometimes tired at the end of the day?
4. How were some other foreigners different from her?
5. How does she suggest dealing with homesickness?
6. How does she deal with comments about her that she doesn't like?

VOCABULARY
Phrasal verbs (1)

1 Complete these sentences from the blog. Use the correct form of the phrasal verbs from the list, then go back to the blog to check your answers.

put up with | bring about | run into | turn out
hang out with | pick up | go through | wear out

1. You have to _____ a lot of new vocabulary.
2. Being homesick is a phase that you have to _____.
3. It's not nice to hear people criticise you, but you have to _____ it.
4. Sometimes you miss the friends you used to _____.
5. Speaking another language all day _____ me _____.
6. Living abroad is _____ to be a great experience for me.
7. I _____ some people who wanted to leave France.
8. Living abroad can _____ some challenges and difficulties.

Pronunciation
Phrasal verb stress
Go to page 120.

2 GOING PLACES

2 Which of the phrasal verbs means:

0 make (someone) very tired — *wear out*
1 meet (without having arranged to) _____
2 learn (informally) _____
3 tolerate _____
4 experience (a difficult situation) _____
5 have a particular result _____
6 spend time with _____
7 make happen _____

3 Answer the questions.

1 Where do you like to hang out? And who with?
2 What wears you out?
3 Have you ever run into a teacher outside school?
4 Can you think of any habits someone you know has that you have to put up with?
5 What difficulties does someone have to go through when they leave school and start university?
6 Do you think it's possible to pick up new words from listening to English-language songs?

> Workbook page 20

GRAMMAR
Omitting relative pronouns

1 Read the two sentences from the blog. Where can you put *that* in each sentence? Is *that* the subject or object of the relative clause? Then complete the rule with the words *subject* and *object*.

1 It's a phase you have to go through.
2 I concentrate on the nice people I meet.

> **RULE:** When the relative pronouns *that* / *which* / *who* are the ¹_____ of a defining relative clause, they can be omitted. But if they are the ²_____ of the defining relative clause, they can't be omitted.

2 Read these sentences. Put a tick (✓) if you can omit the pronoun in *italics*, or a cross (✗) if you can't omit it.

1 You'll miss the friends *who* you used to hang out with.
2 I ran into some people *who* couldn't wait to leave.
3 I've decided to write about some of the challenges *that* living abroad can bring.
4 You become one of those people *who* wish they'd stayed at home.
5 There's new vocabulary *which* you have to pick up.
6 There's no country in the world *that* suits everybody.

Reduced relative clauses

3 Read these sentences. Where could you put the words *that is* and *who is*? Then tick the correct box in the rule.

1 I'm a student living and studying in France.
2 The experience gained by living abroad is invaluable.

> **RULE:** When relative clauses begin with a relative pronoun + the auxiliary verb *be*, we can omit:
> A ☐ only the relative pronoun
> B ☐ the relative pronoun + the verb *be*.

4 Cross out the words / phrases in *italics* that can be left out.

Footballers ¹*who* come from other countries to play in the UK often have problems. Some of the players ²*who are* playing in the UK now are quite young and so they easily feel homesick. And then there are things like food – people ³*who were* brought up on spicy food or exotic fruit don't always like typical British food. But the biggest problems ⁴*that* they face seem to be the weather and the language. The country ⁵*that* they come from might be very hot, which the UK isn't. It isn't always easy for players ⁶*who* come from Brazil or Mexico, for example, to adapt to the grey skies and short winter days ⁷*that* they experience in England. And not all the foreign players learn English very well – the ones ⁸*who* do, tend to find it easier to adapt.

> Workbook page 19

THINK VALUES
Learning from other cultures

1 Imagine you live in another country. Put the things in Becca's blog (A, B, C, D, E) in order (1 = the most difficult, 5 = the least difficult).

1 ☐ 2 ☐ 3 ☐ 4 ☐ 5 ☐

2 Choose the options that are true for you in these statements. Make notes about your reasons.

1 I'd like / I wouldn't like to visit other countries.
2 I'd like / I wouldn't like to live in another country.
3 I'm interested / I'm not interested in other cultures.
4 Knowing about other cultures helps / doesn't help me understand my own culture.
5 I think / I don't think it's good to have people from other countries living in my country.

3 SPEAKING Compare your ideas about Exercises 1 and 2 with the class. How similar or different are you?

Culture

1 Look at the photos. What do they all have in common?
2 🔊 1.15 Read and listen to the article and check your answers.

Nomadic People

Most of us are used to living in the same place – every day, all year round, we go 'home'. But for some people around the world, home is a place that moves. Here are three groups of people who have a nomadic way of life.

1 The Tuareg

In the central part of northern Africa, which is mostly desert, you can find the Tuareg people, who call themselves 'Imohag', meaning 'free people'. Most of the Tuareg people are found in Mali, Niger and Algeria, although some can also be found in Libya and Burkina Faso. However, being nomadic people, they regularly cross national borders.

They have their own language (Tuareg), which is spoken by around 1.2 million people, but many Tuareg people also speak Arabic and/or French. The Tuareg people are mostly Muslim, although some traditional beliefs remain from before the arrival of Islam.

In the past, the Tuareg people moved around the desert areas with their cattle, mainly between places where water could be found. Due to the formation of new countries and stricter borders, severe droughts and urbanisation, nomadic life became more difficult in the 20th century. This led many Tuareg people to settle in towns and cities.

Sometimes the Tuareg people are called 'the blue people of the Sahara', because of the blue turbans that the men wear, which often gives their skin a blue colour.

2 The Shahsavan

This tribe lives in an area of northwest Iran and eastern Azerbaijan. There are approximately 100,000 of them. In the spring, the Shahsavan move from their winter home in Azerbaijan to their camps near Mount Sabalan, about 200 kilometres south, for the summer. Their journey usually takes around three or four weeks. Each day, they travel from midnight to midday, when the heat begins to prevent further travel. Traditionally, the women and children travelled on camels, and the men rode horses or walked, but increasingly the Shahsavan are using lorries and tractors.

When they reach their destination, everyone (including children) is involved in setting up the main camp, consisting of various types of tent. They stay there until September, when the return journey begins.

Many of the Shahsavan believe that their way of life is dying out, that their grandchildren will not do the annual migration any more.

3 Aborigines

The Aboriginal people of Australia have been living there for 40,000 years, since long before Europeans arrived. But they are not one single group – for example, there are over 200 different languages spoken by the Aborigines.

The Aborigines are hunters and gatherers, almost always on the move. Principally it is the women who gather food and care for children, while the men are the hunters. They have very few possessions, and the ones they have are mostly light, since they need to keep moving in search of food and to maintain a balanced diet (they eat seeds, fruit and vegetables, as well as small animals, snakes and insects).

However, they occasionally decide to settle somewhere and form villages.

2 GOING PLACES

3 According to the article, which group (or groups):

1. only travels twice a year?
2. doesn't own many things?
3. speaks more than one language?
4. sometimes lives together in villages?
5. moves from one country to another?
6. has seen their lifestyle change?

4 **VOCABULARY** Match the highlighted words in the article to the definitions.

1. the places where one country ends and another begins
2. on a journey or trip, the place you want to get to
3. all the things that you eat
4. times when it doesn't rain and there is little or no water
5. mainly
6. things that people have and keep
7. that happens once every year
8. stay, continue

SPEAKING

Work with a partner. Discuss the following questions.

1. Do you know of any other groups of people who are nomadic? What do you know about their culture?
2. What do you think might be the advantages and disadvantages of a nomadic lifestyle?
3. The article says that many of the Shahsavan believe that their grandchildren won't live in the same way. Why do you think that might be?

WRITING
An informal email

1 Read Karen's email and answer the questions.

1. How long has she been with the Inuit people?
2. When did she try to catch a seal?
3. What does she say strikes her most about the Inuit?

2 Which word or phrase in the email means:

1. a great deal
2. I have finally arrived
3. agreed that I could accompany them
4. I am extremely happy
5. my experiences here
6. one or two days ago

Hi James,

How are you doing? Hope you're OK!

Well, here I am at last – living in northern Canada with the nomadic Inuit people. You know that I've been wanting to do this for years, and my dream has finally come true. I'm over the moon to be here.

I got here ten days ago and met a family who said I could go along with them to hunt. I've already done some amazing things – sleeping in an igloo, for example, and watching the Inuit people go hunting for fish and for small animals.

The most difficult thing to deal with, of course, is the cold. There's also the fact that you have to keep moving every few days to find food. The way they hunt is interesting. The Inuit make a hole in the ice and hope that a seal will appear so that they can catch it. I went hunting with my host dad a couple of days ago – he showed me how to make a hole and then we stood for six hours in the freezing cold, waiting for a seal to appear. It never came. I got so fed up. But then I thought: 'Hey, the Inuit people do this every day, sometimes waiting for ten hours. And sometimes they catch a seal, and sometimes they don't. What's my problem?' What amazes me most about them is their patience, and my own is getting loads better!

Well, I'll write and tell you more about how I'm getting on with things when I can. Hope you're well!

All the best,

Karen.

---

3 Why does Karen not use the expressions in Exercise 2 in her email?

4 Imagine you are spending two weeks living with one of the nomadic tribes mentioned in the article.

- Choose which of the three groups you are living with.
- Decide what things in general have been good / not so good about your experiences so far.
- Decide on one specific thing about their life that has really impressed you.

5 You're going to write an email to an English-speaking friend.

- Make sure to start and end your email appropriately.
- Talk generally about your experiences first. Then move on to more specific details.
- Write 150–200 words.
- Check your writing to make sure that your language is not formal.

CAMBRIDGE ENGLISH: First

THiNK EXAMS

READING AND USE OF ENGLISH
Part 4: Key word transformations

Workbook page 17

1 For questions 1–6 complete the second sentence so that it has a similar meaning to the first sentence, using the word given. Do not change the word given. You must use between two and five words, including the word given. Here is an example (0).

0   I think taking the 8 pm train is the best idea.
    PREFER
    I'd *prefer to take* the 8 pm train.

1   I've been studying all day and I'm really tired.
    ME
    Studying all day has really _____ out.

2   I wish I hadn't gone to bed so late.
    REGRET
    I _____ to bed so late.

3   I got really annoyed by Paul and Dave laughing all the time.
    WHICH
    Paul and Dave kept laughing, _____ me.

4   I don't know how you tolerate him.
    PUT
    I don't know how you _____ him.

5   Oh no! I didn't post my letter on the way home.
    FORGOT
    I _____ my letter on the way home.

6   Getting up early in the morning is the worst thing.
    STAND
    I _____ up early in the morning.

WRITING
Part 2: An article

Workbook page 25

2   You have seen this announcement in an international teenage magazine.

Write your article in 140–190 words.

TEST YOURSELF — UNITS 1 & 2

VOCABULARY

1 Complete the sentences with the words in the list. There are four extra words.

refugees | turned out | wandering | puzzled | stuck | residents | guilty
staff | rushing | go through | motorists | ran into | worn out | crawl

1 Sally was _____ slowly around the shop looking for a present for her mum's birthday.
2 I hadn't seen Marie for ages, but yesterday I _____ her at the cinema.
3 I saw a documentary about _____ fleeing across borders to escape the war.
4 I'm so happy that I passed my driving test. It was awful and I wouldn't want to _____ that again!
5 You haven't done anything wrong – you don't have to feel _____ about anything, OK?
6 Mr Sawyer runs a small business. He has a _____ of four people.
7 They are all local _____. Most of them live in the streets near us.
8 My little sister can't walk yet, but she can _____ really fast!
9 I was _____ by my friend's reaction – I couldn't understand why she laughed.
10 The beginning of the film was very sad, but it all _____ well in the end.

/10

GRAMMAR

2 Complete the sentences. Use the verbs in the list, either with *to* + infinitive, or with a gerund (*-ing* form). Use two of the verbs twice.

do | go | live | fall

1 Yesterday my friends decided _____ to the beach to play volleyball.
2 My brother says he remembers _____ out of bed when he was two years old.
3 Jack always forgets _____ his homework and then gets in trouble.
4 I want _____ in Paris one day.
5 I don't mind _____ the washing up at home.
6 I hate being in an empty house. I can't imagine _____ alone.

3 Find and correct the mistake in each sentence.

1 I really like that guy which plays Sam on TV.
2 My brother Julian that lives in New York is coming to stay with me.
3 It isn't a film makes everyone laugh.
4 The man what plays the drums in the band is on the left in the photo.
5 My brother broke my phone, what means he has to buy me a new one.
6 She's the runner won the gold medal.

/12

FUNCTIONAL LANGUAGE

4 Choose the correct options.

1 A Next week Rebecca's going to run a 15-kilometre race. That's *quite a / really* distance.
　 B Yes, it is. And she only started running a month ago, too. That's *amazing / daring*.
2 A I heard that you got 95%. That's *OK / phenomenal*. Well done!
　 B Thanks. I could hardly believe it. And my parents thought it was *incredible / quite*.
3 A *I'm betting / bet* you can't say 'Good morning' in five different languages.
　 B Well, you're right – of course I *can / can't*.
4 A You *can / will* never manage to stay off the Internet for two days.
　 B Mm, I think you're right, but I *dare / can dare* you to stop using email for a week!

/8

MY SCORE /30

22 – 30
10 – 21
0 – 9

3 | THE NEXT GENERATION

OBJECTIVES

FUNCTIONS: emphasising
GRAMMAR: quantifiers; *so* and *such* (review); *do* and *did* for emphasis
VOCABULARY: costumes and uniforms; bringing up children

A

B

C

READING

1 Look at the photos and match them with the captions.

☐ King for a day
☐ Go Chargers!
☐ Kiss the chef
☐ Batman and Boy Wonder

2 **SPEAKING** Work in pairs. These photos are all from a blog. What do you think the blog is about?

3 🔊 1.16 Read and listen and check your answers.

4 Read the blog again and answer the questions.

1 What did Rain's parents do on his first day at high school?
2 How many days did Rain's dad, Dale wave at the bus?
3 Which other family members got involved?
4 What were the first and last costumes that Dale wore?
5 How much did Dale spend on the costumes?
6 How did he keep the cost so low?
7 What did Rain think about his dad dressing up at the beginning? And at the end?
8 What does Dale plan to do next term?

5 **SPEAKING** Work in pairs and answer the questions.

1 Does Dale sound like a good dad? Explain your reasons.
2 How would you feel if your dad was like Dale? Why?
3 Why do you think Dale wanted to dress up?

3 THE NEXT GENERATION

■ TRAIN TO THiNK

Changing your opinions

It can be a mistake to believe something just because it's based on an opinion you've formed. Becoming a critical thinker means continually reflecting on our opinions, and keeping them only if they are based on evidence that is true.

1 **Which people from the story may have had the following opinions at some point? Write their names.**

   1 'My dad is the most embarrassing person in the world.' ....
   2 'Rain's dad is really silly.' ....
   3 'I don't think Dale should do this; it's going to cost a lot of money.' ....

2 **SPEAKING** Discuss how the people's opinions in Exercise 1 have changed and why.

> *Initially, Rain thought that his dad was the most embarrassing dad in the world. But with time, he realised that maybe that wasn't true. He learnt to appreciate his dad's sense of humour.*

3 **SPEAKING** Think of opinions that you or family members have had and that have changed. Think about music, school, fashion, friends, etc. Discuss in groups.

An Embarrassing Dad

If you think you have the world's most embarrassing dad, then think again.

American teenager Rain Price has just spent the last half year with his dad waving him off to school from the bus stop outside his house. OK, so that doesn't sound too bad, but this was no ordinary goodbye because each day Rain's dad said goodbye wearing a different fancy-dress costume!

It all started on 16-year-old Rain's first day at high school. Like many proud parents, Rochelle and Dale, Rain's mum and dad, sent him off to school with a big wave from the doorstep. That evening Rain made the mistake of complaining about how embarrassing they were, which gave Dale a great idea.

The next morning as Rain stepped onto the bus outside his house, he could hear all of his school friends laughing at something. He turned around and to his horror, there was his dad waving him off, dressed as an American football player, complete with ball and helmet. But that was just the beginning. For the next 180 school days, come rain or shine, Dale waved goodbye to his son dressed in a different costume. One day he was a king waving his sword and shield, the next a chef in his hat and apron, the following a pirate. Then there was Elvis and Wonder Woman. Dale even got other members of the family involved, using Rain's younger brother to play Batman alongside his Robin.

Amazingly Dale only spent $50 on all of his costumes. He got loads of costumes from the family fancy-dress collection and then there were several friends and neighbours happy to help.

Some of Rain's friends didn't find it funny but most of them looked forward to seeing what Dale would be wearing. And Dale also found an international audience for his dressing up too, as each day Rochelle took a photo of her husband in fancy dress and put it on their blog, waveatthebus.blogspot.com, which became a hit on the Internet. Even Rain was eventually able to see the funny side and realised that his dad was pretty cool after all.

But all good things must come to an end and for the final farewell on the last day of school, Dale dressed up as a pirate and stood next to a sign reading 'It's been fun waving at the bus. Have a great summer'. He has no plans to wave Rain off to school next year. Instead, he's looking forward to getting a little more sleep each morning.

GRAMMAR
Quantifiers

1 **Look back at the blog and complete the sentences. Then read the rule and complete the table with** *loads of, a little, all, several* **and** *none*.

1 Like _____ proud parents …
2 He could hear _____ of his school friends laughing at something.
3 He got _____ of costumes from the family fancy-dress collection.
4 There were _____ friends and neighbours happy to help.
5 _____ of his friends didn't find it funny but _____ of them looked forward to it.
6 He's looking forward to getting a _____ more sleep each morning.

> **RULE:** Quantifiers are words and expressions that we use to talk about amount.
>
> 0%   1 _____
>   hardly any
>   a few / 2 _____, not many / much, a small number of
>   some / 3 _____
>   4 _____ / a lot of, lots of, plenty, much / many, a good deal of
>   most, almost all, the vast majority of
> 100% 5 _____

2 **Choose the correct options.**

1 I've got *a few / loads of* followers on my blog – more than 200.
2 I spend *a lot of / hardly any* time with my friends – we meet up every day after school and most weekends too.
3 I spend *most / hardly any* of my time on my tablet. It's the most important thing I've got.
4 *A small number / Most* of my teachers are really nice. I really like this school.
5 *Most / All* of my family live near me, but I've got an uncle who lives in Australia.
6 I spend *almost all / hardly any* of my money on downloads. I don't really care about music.

3 **SPEAKING** Discuss the sentences in Exercise 2 in pairs. Which of them are true for you?

→ Workbook page 28

VOCABULARY
Costumes and uniforms

1 **Look back at the photos of Dale. Which of these things can you see? Write the number next to the words. There are two things which aren't in the photos. Check their meaning.**

☐ sword and shield   ☐ helmet
☐ leather jacket   ☐ cape
☐ wig   ☐ mask
☐ belt   ☐ apron
☐ sunglasses   ☐ football top

2 **Look at the photos. Who is wearing a costume? Who is wearing a uniform? Who is wearing a kit?**

A

B

C

3 **SPEAKING** Discuss in pairs.

1 Do you or does anybody you know wear a uniform? Describe it.
2 Can you list five jobs in which people wear uniforms?
3 Describe a sports kit to your partner, but don't say what sport it's for. Can your partner guess?
4 Describe your perfect costume to wear to a fancy-dress party.

→ Workbook page 30

3 THE NEXT GENERATION

LISTENING

1 🔊 1.17 **Listen and match the names of the places with the pictures.**

France | Poland | Britain | Japan
Mexico | Argentina

Introduce them early

Keep it in the family

No time for bedtime

Let them solve their own problems

Early to bed

Young chefs

2 🔊 1.17 **Listen again and choose the correct answers.**

1 Why do many parents feel guilty about the way they bring up their children?
   A They don't give their children enough attention.
   B They feel they are too strict.
   C They don't always do what they think they should do.

2 What did Miriam notice about Argentinian children?
   A They are often more tired, especially in the morning.
   B They often sleep too much and so are unable to get to sleep early.
   C They begin developing social skills when they are very young.

3 Why does Miriam feel French children are better eaters?
   A Their parents encourage them to try all sorts of food.
   B They are expected to like all foods from an early age.
   C French cooking is better than British cooking.

4 What surprised Miriam in the Japanese school?
   A The children weren't always well-behaved.
   B The teacher was happy to let the children argue in class.
   C How good the teacher was at helping the children sort out their problems.

5 What does the speaker feel is the most important thing we can learn from *Bringing up Babies*?
   A British people aren't bringing up their children as well as parents in other places.
   B Bringing up children isn't easy.
   C We can learn a lot about parenting from people in other countries.

THiNK SELF-ESTEEM

Developing independence

1 Read each sentence and choose a number from 1–5 (1 = I strongly agree, 5 = I strongly disagree.)

1 Teenagers should set their own bedtimes. 1 2 3 4 5
2 Teenagers should have a part-time job to earn their own pocket money. 1 2 3 4 5
3 Teenagers should choose what they eat. 1 2 3 4 5
4 Teenagers should spend weekends with parents / family. 1 2 3 4 5
5 Teenagers should help around the house. 1 2 3 4 5

2 **SPEAKING** Discuss your answers in small groups. Which question(s) do almost all of you agree on? And which one(s) do almost all of you disagree on? Why?

READING

1. Look at the book cover. What kind of book do you think it is? Read the introduction to find out.

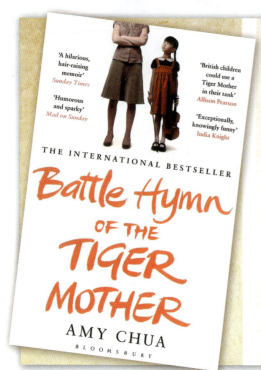

Many people wonder how Chinese parents bring up such successful children. They wonder what Chinese parents do to produce so many mathematical and musical geniuses, what it's like inside the family, and if they could do it too. Well, Amy Chua can tell them, because she's done it.

* * *

Her daughters, Sophia and Louisa were polite, intelligent and helpful. They were two years ahead of their classmates in Maths and had amazing musical abilities. But Sophia and Louisa weren't allowed to spend a night at a friend's house, be in a school play, choose what they wanted to do after school, or get any grade lower than an A.

* * *

In *Battle Hymn of the Tiger Mother*, Amy Chua tells of her experiences bringing up her children the 'Chinese way'. It is a story about a mother and two daughters and two very different cultures. Funny, entertaining and provocative, this is an important book that will change your ideas about parenting forever.

2. Read these two opinions from readers of Amy Chua's book. Which one is 'for' and which one is 'against' the Tiger mum style of parenting? What reasons do they give?

For and against – Tiger Mums

This is an interesting book but Amy Chua's parenting ideas are too strict for me. For example, Tiger mums don't let their children watch any TV or play any computer games. How can any child in the 21st Century grow up without playing on a computer? What is she trying to do? Take away their childhoods?

I do understand that she feels she was only doing the best for her children and trying to help them get ahead in life. But there are loads of children who spend hours in front of the TV and still do well.

Stephanie, 15

I think Amy Chua's ideas are fantastic. Yes, she was hard on her children at times but she did bring up two amazing children. Her daughters are so confident, they'll do really well in life.

Too many parents are soft on their children these days. They use the TV as a way of keeping them quiet. They don't have enough time for their children. My mum and dad are strict and they don't let me do a lot of things my friends do. It is hard at times, but they are always there when I need help with my school work or have a problem with other students at school. They are just trying to do their best for me.

Tim, 16

3. Read the texts again. Who might say these things? Write Amy, Stephanie or Tim.
   1. I talk about my problems with my parents.
   2. No, you can't sleep at Chloe's house.
   3. Children need to be free to make some of their own decisions.
   4. My parents don't let me watch much TV, but that's OK.
   5. You'll thank me one day.
   6. You can't make children be what you want them to be.

SPEAKING

Work in pairs and answer the questions.
1. Who do you agree with most, Tim or Stephanie? Why?
2. Can you think of any other examples of rules that strict parents have?

3 THE NEXT GENERATION

GRAMMAR
so and such (review)

1 Write the correct words to complete the sentences. Check in the texts, then complete the rule with *so* and *such*.

1 Her daughters are _____ confident, they'll do really well in life.
2 Many people wonder how Chinese parents bring up _____ successful children.

> **RULE:** We use *so* and *such* to emphasise.
> ¹_____ (*a/an*) + (adjective) + noun
> ²_____ + adjective
>
> We often follow *so* and *such* with a *that* clause to talk about consequences.
> *It was such a difficult question that I didn't know what to say.*
> *It was so hot that I couldn't sunbathe.*

2 Complete with *so* or *such* and then complete the sentences with your own ideas.

0 It was *such* a hot day that *we stopped working and went to the beach*.
1 The homework was _____ difficult that …
2 He's _____ a good friend that …
3 The train was _____ late that …
4 It was _____ an exciting book that …

do and did for emphasis

3 Complete the sentences from the texts with the missing word, then read the rule.

1 I _____ understand that she feels she was only doing the best for her children.
2 She was hard on her children at times but she _____ bring up two amazing children.

> **RULE:** We can use the auxiliaries *do*, *does*, *did* to add emphasis to what we want to say, often when we're contradicting someone.
> *You didn't like the film, did you? I **did** like the film!*
> *She doesn't want to go to the party. She **does** want to go – she's just shy.*

> **LOOK!** *Too* and *(not) enough*
> To say something is more than we need, we use *too* and to say that it's less we use *not enough*.
> *too* + adjective
> *too* + *many* + countable noun
> *too* + *much* + uncountable noun
> *not* + adjective + *enough*

4 Complete the second sentence so it has a similar meaning to the first sentence, using the word given and *so/such*, *did* for emphasis and *too / (not) enough*. Write between 2 and 5 words.

1 There were too many people at the meeting. Some people had to stand.
There _____ at the meeting that some people had to stand. (chairs)
2 He spends too much money.
He _____ money. (save)
3 This book isn't interesting enough. I'm not going to finish it. This book is _____ finish. (boring)
4 You're wrong. I thought the book was really, really good.
I _____ the book. (like)
5 I really think we should leave now.
I _____ stay. (shouldn't)

Workbook page 28

Pronunciation
Adding emphasis
Go to page 120.

VOCABULARY
Bringing up children

1 Complete the text with the words in the list.

bring | strict | do | soft
childhood | do | get | grow

The toughest job in the world
Most parents want to ¹_____ *their best* for their children and help them ²_____ *ahead in life*. They try to ³_____ their children up well and give them a happy ⁴_____. But it's not always so easy. Children ⁵_____ up so fast these days and it can be difficult to get it right all the time. Of course, parents know the importance of school and they want their children to ⁶_____ *well* but what happens when the child doesn't want to try? If they are too ⁷_____, their children might rebel. If they are too ⁸_____ then the children might only do the things they want to do. It's a difficult balancing act and, of course, parents get it wrong sometimes. After all, they're only human too.

2 Match the expressions a–h in the text with their meanings.

a make advances in life
b raise
c get older
d be a success
e to describe a parent who has very few (or no) rules
f be as good as you can
g to describe a parent who has lots of rules
h the time of being a child

Workbook page 30

Literature

1 Look at the photo and then read the introduction to the extract. How do you think Marcus feels about his relationship with his mum?

2 🔊 1.20 Read and listen to the extract and check your ideas.

About a Boy by Nick Hornby

Marcus is a schoolboy who lives with his mum, who is depressed. Marcus has a bad time at school – he gets bullied quite a lot, especially because of the clothes his mum makes him wear. Marcus has met Will, a rich lazy man who makes friends with Marcus and buys him new trainers.

Here, Marcus and his mum are going home after visiting Will at his flat.

'You're not going round there again,' she said on the way home.
  Marcus knew she'd say it, and he also knew that he'd take no notice, but he argued anyway.
  'Why not?'
  'If you've got anything to say, you say it to me. If you want new clothes, I'll get them.'
  'But you don't know what I need.'
  'So tell me.'
  'I don't know what I need. Only Will knows what I need.'
  'Don't be ridiculous.'
  'It's true. He knows what things kids wear.'
  'Kids wear what they put on in the mornings.'
  'You know what I mean.'
  'You mean that he thinks he's trendy, and that […] he knows which trainers are fashionable, even though he doesn't know the first thing about anything else.'
  That was exactly what he meant. That was what Will was good at, and Marcus thought he was lucky to have found him.
  'We don't need that kind of person. We're doing all right our way.'
  Marcus looked out of the bus window and thought about whether this was true, and decided it wasn't, that neither of them were doing all right, whichever way you looked at it.
  'If you are having trouble it's nothing to do with what shoes you wear, I can tell you that for nothing.'
  'No, I know, but –'
  'Marcus, trust me, OK? I've been your mother for twelve years. I haven't made too bad a job of it. I do think about it. I know what I'm doing.'
  Marcus had never thought of his mother in that way before, as someone who knew what she was doing. He had never thought that she didn't have a clue either; it was just that what she did with him (for him? to him?) didn't appear to be anything like that. He had always looked on being a mother as straightforward, something like, say, driving: most people could do it, and you could mess it up by doing something really obvious, by driving your car into a bus, or not telling your kid to say please and thank you and sorry (there were loads of kids at school, he reckoned, kids who stole and swore too much and bullied other kids, whose mums and dads had a lot to answer for). If you looked at it that way, there wasn't an awful lot to think about. But his mum seemed to be saying that there was more to it than that. She was telling him she had a plan.
  If she had a plan, then he had a choice. He could trust her, believe her when she said she knew what she was doing […] Or he could decide that, actually, she was off her head […] Either way it was scary. He didn't want to put up with things as they were, but the other choice meant he'd have to be his own mother, and how could you be your own mother when you were only twelve? He could tell himself to say please and thank you and sorry, that was easy, but he didn't know where to start with the rest of it. He didn't even know what the rest of it was. He hadn't even known until today that there was a rest of it.

3 Read the extract again. Find the part of the text which tells us that Marcus …

1. is 12 years old.
2. and his mother are not walking home.
3. thinks that both he and his mother have problems.
4. begins to see his mother differently.
5. doesn't think very highly of some of the kids at his school.
6. is happy that he has met Will.

4 VOCABULARY Match the highlighted words in the extract with the definitions.

1. up-to-date with modern fashion
2. do it in a really bad way
3. knows nothing at all
4. simple; not complicated
5. give advice for free
6. used bad words (words that people think are rude)
7. crazy
8. no matter how

5 SPEAKING Work in pairs. Discuss the questions.

1. What do you think Marcus means when he talks about 'the rest of it' in the last two sentences?
2. Do you think that being a mother or father is straightforward? Why (not)?

FUNCTIONS
Emphasising

1 Add *so*, *such*, *do* or *did* to the sentences to make them more emphatic and make any other necessary changes.

1. He's a good father.
2. She gets on well with children.
3. She's patient.
4. My dad tried his best.
5. My parents made some mistakes.
6. She's soft on her children.
7. He's a strict father.
8. Parents get it wrong sometimes.

2 Work in pairs. Who might be talking to whom in each of the sentences in Exercise 1? What was said before? Discuss.

3 WRITING Choose one of the sentences and develop it into a six-line dialogue. The sentence you choose from Exercise 1 could appear at the beginning, middle or end of your dialogue.

4 Think about someone you know who is really good with children or teenagers. Make notes.

Think about:
- their personality
- ways in which they are good with children

5 Work in pairs. Talk about the person. Give examples and use emphasis when you can.

WRITING
An essay

Choose one of the titles below and write an essay.

- Parents always know best
- Children need rules

Remember to:
- write a short introduction to the topic
- give two or three points with examples to support the statement
- give two or three points with examples to argue against the statement
- conclude, giving your opinion

Write your essay in 160–200 words.

4 THINKING OUTSIDE THE BOX

OBJECTIVES

FUNCTIONS: expressing frustration
GRAMMAR: *be / get used to (doing)* vs. *used to (do)*; adverbs and adverbial phrases
VOCABULARY: personality adjectives; common adverbial phrases

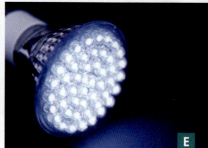

READING

1 Look at the photos. Match the photos with these words:
- lions
- cattle
- a scarecrow
- a light bulb
- a battery
- a solar panel

2 **SPEAKING** Work in pairs or small groups. There are people in a tribe in Africa who want to stop lions killing their cows. Think of ways they could do this using the items in the photos.

3 Read the article and match summaries A–F with the sections 1–5. There is one extra summary.

A The lions are finally fooled
B An accidental light on the problem
C Some success with scarecrows
D The dilemma of the Masai people
E The outcomes for animals and the inventor
F An idea that didn't quite work

4 Read the article again. Seven sentences have been removed. Choose from A–H the sentence which fits each gap (1–7). There is one extra sentence.

A But that didn't work at all – in fact, it seemed that the fire actually lit up the cowsheds and made life easier for the lions.
B After a night or two, they got used to seeing this motionless thing and realised it posed no danger.
C Richard's creativity also led to him winning a scholarship at one of the top schools in Kenya.
D The lions kept well away.
E He connected everything up to some light bulbs, which he then put outside the cowshed.
F They went in to kill the cattle.
G Richard, a responsible young man, felt terrible about it and decided he had to do something to keep the lions out without killing them.
H It has also given him the pleasure of seeing people and cattle and lions living together without the conflict that used to exist in the past.

5 🔊 1.21 Listen and check your answers to Exercise 4. Were your predictions in Exercise 2 right?

6 **SPEAKING** In pairs or small groups, do the following.

1 On a scale of 1–5 agree on how impressive you think Richard's invention is. (1 = not impressive at all, 5 = brilliant!) Say why your group has given this score.
2 Richard gave a talk about his invention. Imagine you were in the audience. Think of two questions you would ask him at the end of his talk.

4 THINKING OUTSIDE THE BOX

Lion Lights

1. Richard Turere is a member of the Masai tribe who live in Central and East Africa. The Masai are traditionally farmers and often keep cattle, an important source of food and income for them. But a problem is that lions sometimes come to the farms and kill the cattle. The Masai are used to lions attacking their livestock, but of course they aren't happy about it. The only solution seemed to be to kill the lions and this had some degree of success in terms of protecting their cattle, but the Masai weren't very happy about doing that, either, because they were reducing the population of lions.

2. In the Masai tribe the young boys are responsible for protecting their fathers' cattle. One day, when Richard was 11, he woke up and found that a lion had killed his father's only bull. ^{1}_____.

   His first idea was to use fire, on the basis that lions were probably scared of fire. ^{2}_____. So Richard had to come up with something else.

3. His next idea was to use a scarecrow. Richard hoped that he could trick the lions into thinking that there was a person there, but lions are pretty clever. ^{3}_____. And then they went in to attack the farm animals.

   Then one night, Richard spent hours walking around in the cowshed with a torch. That night, no lions came, so he worked out that they were afraid of the moving light. And, being imaginative, he had an idea.

4. Richard is a bright young man who used to play with things to see how they worked, and he learned a lot about electrical gadgets that way. So he got a battery and a solar panel to charge it, and then he got an indicator box from an old motorcycle – the box that makes a light blink, to show if the biker is turning left or right. ^{4}_____. The bulbs flashed throughout the night, and the lions thought that someone was walking around inside the cowshed when in fact everyone was in bed asleep. ^{5}_____.

5. Since Richard invented his 'lion lights', his father has not lost any more cattle to lion attacks. And now Richard's idea is being used in many different places, to keep lions, leopards and elephants away from farms and homes for good. ^{6}_____. He was also invited to talk at a conference in the USA. ^{7}_____.

TRAIN TO THiNK

Lateral thinking

1 Read the example.

'Lateral thinking' means solving problems by thinking in a creative way. It means not following the obvious line of thinking. Here is an example.

A woman is driving down a city street at 25 miles per hour. The speed limit is 30 miles per hour. She passes three cars that are travelling at 20 miles per hour. A police officer stops her and gives her a £100 fine. Why?

If we think too much about the speed, we may not get the answer. What does the situation NOT tell us? It doesn't tell us, for example, what time of day it is – so a possible reason for the £100 fine is that it is night time and the woman is driving with no lights on her car. Or another possible reason for the fine is that the street is one-way, and the woman is driving the wrong way.

2 SPEAKING Work in pairs or small groups. Here are more situations. See if you can find possible answers.

1. A father and son are in a bad car crash. They are both taken to hospital. The son is taken into the operating theatre. The doctor there looks at the boy and says: 'That's my son!' *How is this possible?*

2. A woman is lying awake in bed. She dials a number on the phone, says nothing, puts the phone down and then goes to sleep. *Why?*

3. A man lives on the twelfth floor of a building. Every morning, he takes the lift down to the entrance and leaves the building. In the evening, he gets into the lift, and, if there is someone else in the lift, he goes directly to the twelfth floor. If the lift is empty, he goes to the tenth floor and walks up two flights of stairs to his apartment. *Why?*

39

GRAMMAR
be / get used to (doing) vs. used to (do)

1 **Complete these sentences about the article on page 39 with the words in the list. Then complete the rule by choosing the correct options.**

play | exist | attacking | seeing

1 A conflict used to _____ between the farmers and the lions.
2 The Masai are used to lions _____ their livestock.
3 The lions got used to _____ the scarecrow.
4 Richard used to _____ with things to see how they worked.

> **RULE:** We use:
> - ¹*used to do / be used to doing* to talk about situations that were true in the past but are not true any more.
> - ²*used to do / be used to doing* to talk about something that is familiar.
> - ³*be used to doing / get used to doing* to talk about the process of something becoming familiar.

2 **Choose the correct options.**

1 When he was a child, Richard used *to look after / to looking after* his father's cattle.
2 The Masai people are used *to hear / to hearing* the sounds of lions at night.
3 The lions have never got used *to see / to seeing* the flashing lights.
4 Richard used *to watch / to watching* planes when they flew over the farm.
5 Richard used *to imagine / to imagining* going on a plane to America.
6 Richard is used *to speak / to speaking* in public now. He's given several talks at conferences.

3 **Complete with the correct form of *be* or *get*.**

1 I'm from Sweden, so I _____ used to cold weather.
2 Did it take you long to _____ used to the food here?
3 I lived in the UK for years, but I never _____ used to driving on the left.
4 I think I'll never _____ used to summer in January!
5 _____ you used to life here now?
6 We didn't eat the food in China at first because we _____ used to it.

4 **SPEAKING** Work with a partner. Find:
- 2 things that both you and your partner used to do
- 2 things you are used to doing
- 2 things that you have got used to this year

Workbook page 36

VOCABULARY
Personality adjectives

1 **Which of the adjectives in the list are used in the article to describe Richard Turere? What do they mean?**

bright | responsible | decisive | bad-tempered
imaginative | organised | impatient | practical
confident | cautious | arrogant | dull

2 **Read about these people Jane met at her new school.**

a Tick (✓) the people she likes. Write (✗) for the people she doesn't like. Write (?) where it isn't clear.

b Complete the spaces with a word from Exercise 1.

0 Brian gets angry all the time and he complains a lot. He's pretty *bad-tempered*. ✗
1 Barbara understands quickly and has lots of good ideas. She's very _____.
2 Carla doesn't like taking risks. She's a very _____ person.
3 Dana's great because she makes her mind up really quickly – a really _____ girl.
4 Derek never has anything interesting to say – he's so _____!
5 Imogen always has wonderful ideas, she's very _____.
6 Ian wants everything and he wants it now! He's pretty _____.
7 Oscar always knows where things are and what he has to do – he's very _____.
8 Rita is someone you can trust, who makes good decisions – she's _____.

Workbook page 38

SPEAKING

1 **Work in pairs. Think of five different people and write sentences to describe them but don't use the adjective.**

> Jo is waiting for her friend, who's two minutes late. She calls her to see where she is.

2 **Change partner and read your sentences. Can they guess the adjective you were thinking of?**

> impatient

3 **Ask your partner extra questions about the adjective.**

> Do you often get impatient in this kind of situation?

4 THINKING OUTSIDE THE BOX

LISTENING
Being imaginative

1 Look at the two tasks. Think of ideas for both. Then compare with a partner.

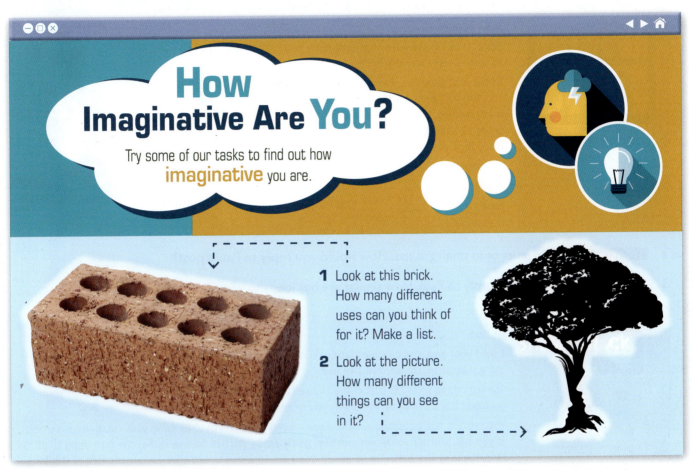

2 **1.22** Briony and Mark did the tasks. Listen to their conversation and answer questions 1 and 2.
   1 Note the six uses Briony thought of for the brick.
   2 Note the four things Mark saw in the picture.

3 **SPEAKING** In groups, compare Briony and Mark's ideas with what you thought of in Exercise 1.

4 **1.22** Listen again and complete each sentence with no more than three words.
   1 Briony only _____ six ideas.
   2 Briony thinks you can put the brick on top of a _____ so that they don't fly away in the wind.
   3 Mark thinks Briony is wrong about using the brick as a hammer to put _____ into a wall.
   4 Briony accuses Mark of _____ when he says he can see a brain.
   5 Mark says the quiz is meant to demonstrate _____ people are.
   6 Briony says that Mark shouldn't be _____ on himself.

THiNK VALUES
Appreciating creative solutions

1 Choose the best way to finish this sentence.

   I think the tasks in Exercise 1 tell us that …

   1 it's important to be imaginative.
   2 being imaginative is better than being practical.
   3 you can be an imaginative person even if you're not good at these tasks.
   4 not everybody is as imaginative as everybody else.
   5 everybody's imagination is different.

2 Now put these in order of importance for you. (1 = most important, 5 = least important)
   - being practical
   - being imaginative
   - knowing a lot of things
   - being responsible
   - being organised

3 **SPEAKING** Work in pairs. Compare your answers in Exercises 1 and 2. How similar are your ideas?

READING

1 Read the post from Paul on the 'Answers4U' website. What problem does he have?

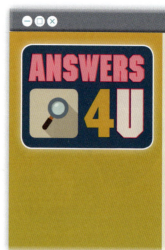

Hello everyone,

I'm 17 and I'm going to start university soon. I'm going to study journalism because I want to work in TV.

In the first semester, everyone has to do a course called 'Creative Thinking and Writing'. At first I thought it wouldn't be a problem – but now I'm really anxious because I'm not a creative person at all! I'm scared that I'm going to look stupid and that I won't pass the course, or else, I'll only get through it with great difficulty.

Can anyone help me? Some tips on being creative would be good!

Thanks a lot!

Paul

2 **SPEAKING** Work in pairs or in small groups. How would you reply to Paul's post?

3 Read what Sarah writes in reply to Paul. How similar are her ideas to yours?

Hi Paul,

I read your post and can completely relate to it. I've been in exactly the same situation – I even did a journalism course, just like you. So here are my thoughts.

The first thing to say is that if the course is any good, it'll start off by helping you with your problem! But I can understand why you're anxious.

You say 'I'm not a creative person'. Look – everyone's creative! Denying your creativity is terrible. If you tell yourself you're not creative, you'll easily start to believe it. So, the first thing to do is: stop thinking like that! I'm no expert but I do want you to see that you are capable of thinking creatively. People sometimes talk about 'thinking outside the box' – you know, thinking in a different way – but actually, the only box is the way we've been brought up to see problems. A central obstacle to our ability to think outside the box is the assumption that there must always be a 'right' answer to a question or problem, and that limits creative thinking. So, try to stop seeing things as 'right' or 'wrong'.

Another problem is this: we come up with an idea and then we immediately think, 'Oh, that's no good.' We criticise our own thoughts and ideas before we give them a chance to grow! While you're thinking, just try to brainstorm ideas in an enjoyable way – then choose the best ideas later.

And don't worry about looking stupid. If you try an idea and other people laugh at it, that's their problem, not yours. Try to look at the course as a way to have fun. Work hard, don't hold yourself back, do everything with enthusiasm and you'll be fine.

Anyway, enough from me. I hope these ideas help.

Sarah

4 Read the letters again. Mark the statements T (true) or F (false).

1 Paul intends to become a newspaper reporter.
2 Paul thinks he is going to fail his course.
3 Paul wants advice about how to be creative.
4 Sarah doesn't get why Paul is worried.
5 Sarah can see why Paul is worried.
6 Sarah believes that it is a bad thing to say you're not creative.
7 Sarah thinks that problems have correct solutions.
8 Sarah thinks people shouldn't criticise their own ideas.

5 **SPEAKING** Work with a partner. Discuss the questions.

1 If you were Paul, would you find Sarah's answer useful? Why (not)?
2 Which of her comments do you like most? Which do you like least?

Pronunciation

Pronouncing words with *gh*
Go to page 120.

4 THINKING OUTSIDE THE BOX

GRAMMAR
Adverbs and adverbial phrases

1 **For each sentence, put a letter in the box to say if the underlined adverb is an adverb of time (T), manner (M), place (P) or certainty (C).**

0 I read your post and can <u>completely</u> relate to it. — **M**
1 I read about it <u>recently</u>.
2 This is <u>definitely</u> the best album they've ever made.
3 He'll <u>probably</u> win the prize.
4 You can buy most of the things you need <u>locally</u>.
5 You are capable of thinking <u>creatively</u>.
6 We got <u>home</u> at nine o'clock.
7 This is <u>possibly</u> the best work I've ever done.
8 You can choose the best ideas <u>later</u>.
9 I applied for the course, and, <u>surprisingly</u>, they accepted me!

2 **Look back at Sarah's reply on page 42. What verbs do these words qualify?**

1 completely   3 creatively   5 hard
2 easily   4 immediately

3 **Sometimes we use adverbial phrases instead of an adverb. Add the words below to lists A and B. Then choose the correct words to complete the rule.**

friendly | interesting | fear | surprise | strange | enthusiasm

A	B
in an enjoyable way	with / without difficulty
in a horrible way	with / without excitement
in a different way	with / without interest
in a _____ way	with / without _____
in an _____ way	with / without _____
in a _____ way	with / without _____

> **RULE:** We often form adverbial phrases with:
> - in a/an + ¹*noun / adjective* way
> - with/without + ²*noun / adjective*

4 **Complete the sentences. Use expressions from Exercise 3. There might be more than one possibility.**

0 I really like football, so I went to the match with <u>interest / enthusiasm / excitement</u>.
1 The first time I met him, he looked at me in _____.
2 The homework was easy – I did it without _____.
3 Some of the people at the party were dressed in _____.
4 It was a great programme and I watched it with _____.
5 I don't really like parties, so I went to Cindy's without _____.

> Workbook page 36

VOCABULARY
Common adverbial phrases

1 **Use words from the list to complete the definitions.**

~~in secret~~ | in a row | on purpose
in a panic | by accident | in a hurry
in private | in public

If you do something …

0 without other people knowing, you do it <u>in secret</u>.
1 that other people can hear or see, you do it _____.
2 that other people can't hear or see, you do it _____.
3 that you intended to do, you do it _____.
4 that you didn't want to do, you do it _____.
5 feeling stressed and without thinking properly, you do it _____.
6 quickly, you do it _____.
7 three times without a break, you do it three times _____.

2 **Choose the correct options to complete the sentences.**

1 The two of us went into a room, alone, so that we could talk *in a hurry / in private*.
2 He broke my phone and I'm really angry. I'm sure he did it *on purpose / in a panic*.
3 You shouldn't have behaved that way *in public / in private*. Everyone was staring.
4 I woke up late four days *in a row / by accident*!
5 I was very late so I had to leave the house *on purpose / in a hurry*.
6 He was *in secret / in a panic* because he couldn't find his mobile phone.
7 I'm so sorry that I lost your papers – I left them on the bus *on purpose / by accident*.
8 She did it late at night *in secret / in a panic*. No one knew anything.

3 **SPEAKING** **Work with a partner. Discuss the questions.**

1 When were you last in a hurry?
2 What can you do five times in a row?
3 Give an example of something you did on purpose, and wish you hadn't.
4 Give an example of something you got right by accident.
5 When was the last time you were in a panic?

> Workbook page 38

43

PHOTOSTORY: episode 2

Writer's block

1 Look at the photos and answer the questions.

1. Look at what the teacher has written on the board. What do you think the homework is?
2. How does Emma feel about the homework?
3. Do you think Justin is being helpful?

2 🔊 1.25 Now read and listen to the photostory. Check your ideas.

TEACHER OK, everyone, so this is what I want you to do by Friday, OK? A short story, of five hundred words.
EMMA Five hundred words!? She can't be serious!
TEACHER ... and the story has to end with the words, 'Thanks, you saved my life!'
EMMA What? This is awful. I can't do that. I'm hopeless at writing stories.
TEACHER It has to be original, though. No using old stories and changing them a bit here and there. I want something that's yours and yours alone. Be creative! OK, end of lesson. Bye!

EMMA And she wants it by Friday! That's the day after tomorrow. I'll never come up with anything by then. An original story? Me? No chance.
LIAM Sounds like you've given up without even trying.
NICOLE Liam's right, Emma. I mean, come on, it can't be that hard, can it?
EMMA An original story, five hundred words long? I think that's pretty hard.
JUSTIN What's the ending again?
EMMA Someone says, 'Thanks, you saved my life!'
JUSTIN OK, that's five words. So far, so good. All you need is another four hundred and ninety-five.
EMMA You know, Justin, I may not be very good at creative writing but I can think of a few words for you right now!
NICOLE OK, calm down.
JUSTIN Well, I'm sorry, Emma. But you know, all you've got to do is think of a story you've read or a film you've seen ...
EMMA No, no, that's just it – it has to be original.
LIAM Well, there must be some stories she's never read.
EMMA You don't know Miss Jenkins. She's read every book, seen every film ...
JUSTIN Why don't you write a story about a girl who's got to write a story, and her friends give her a great idea and then she says 'Thanks, you saved my life!' The hero could be a really cool guy called Justin.
NICOLE Give it a rest, Justin!

EMMA OK, well this isn't getting me anywhere. And I've got to go home. I'm off – I'll see you lot later. And thanks for all the help, Justin! You're a real pal – not.
JUSTIN Hey, what did I do?
LIAM Well, you were a bit out of order, Justin. You can see that Emma's stressed out already, and you didn't exactly help, did you?

4 THINKING OUTSIDE THE BOX

DEVELOPING SPEAKING

3 Work in pairs. Discuss what happens next in the story. Write down your ideas.

We think Emma watches a film and gets an idea.

4 ▶ EP2 Watch to find out how the story continues.

5 Match the sentence beginnings and endings.

1 Emma sees a woman who
2 The woman works for
3 The woman is desperate because
4 Emma tries to help
5 When Emma gets an idea
6 Emma gets the keys out
7 Emma's really happy about

a but she can't get the keys out.
b the last thing the woman says.
c is looking for something.
d using something she got at a shop.
e the owner of an art gallery.
f she goes to a shop nearby.
g she hasn't got a spare set of keys.

PHRASES FOR FLUENCY

1 Find these expressions in the photostory. Who says them? How do you say them in your language?

1 (She) can't be serious.
2 (What's the ending) again?
3 Calm down.
4 That's just it.
5 Give it a rest.
6 (You were a bit) out of order.

2 Use the expressions in Exercise 1 to complete the sentences.

1 I know you told me before, but what's your name _____?
2 A Let's go for a walk in the park.
   B A walk in the park? You _____! It's raining!
3 A Come on, we're late!
   B _____, we're not late at all, we've got another fifteen minutes.
4 A Your hair looks really stupid!
   B Oh, _____, Michelle. I'm tired of how you criticise me all the time. You're really _____, you know?
5 A I don't feel like going out. Let's stay here and watch TV.
   B _____. You never want to go out.

WordWise
Expressions with *good*

1 Use the phrases in the list to complete these sentences from the unit so far.

~~for good~~ | So far, so good | not very good at
It's no good | It's a good thing | it's all good

0 The lights have stopped animals coming to the farm *for good*.
1 I'm _____ creative thinking.
2 That's five words. _____.
3 She gave me an A minus, best I've ever got! So _____.
4 _____. I just can't get the keys out.
5 _____ Emma's such a nice person.

2 Which phrase means:

1 for ever
2 It's not successful.
3 Everything is all right.
4 We have started but not finished, but everything has been OK until now.
5 not talented at
6 I'm/We're/You're lucky that …

➤ Workbook page 38

FUNCTIONS
Expressing frustration

1 Read the photostory again. Which of these things does Emma not say? What do all the sentences have in common?

1 I can't (do that).
2 I'm hopeless (at …)
3 This is hopeless!
4 No chance.
5 I give up.
6 I'll never (come up with anything).
7 This is pointless.

2 Think about the woman who loses her keys. Write three things she might have thought using the expressions in Exercise 1.

I'll never get the keys out.

WRITING
A story

Write a story. The story must end with the words:

'Thanks, you saved my life!'

Write 120–150 words.

CAMBRIDGE ENGLISH: First

THiNK EXAMS

LISTENING
Part 3: Multiple matching

Workbook page 35

1. ◆)) 1.26 You will hear five different people talking about an after-school art group. Choose from the list (A–H) what each speaker likes most about the group. Use the letters only once. There are three extra letters that you do not need to use.

   A It's fun to learn different forms of art.
   B It's good to meet people with the same interest.
   C It's fun to spend more time with your friends.
   D It will be useful for the future.
   E It's interesting to find out about painters from other times.
   F The teacher really helps you achieve good results.
   G It's good to practise sports in a club.
   H It brings out your creative side.

   Speaker 1 ☐
   Speaker 2 ☐
   Speaker 3 ☐
   Speaker 4 ☐
   Speaker 5 ☐

WRITING
Part 2: An email

Workbook page 43

2. You have recently enquired about going on a residential art course for a week. You have received the following reply.

   > Thank you for your email. It sounds like you would be perfect for the course. We offer lessons in all types of art. However, if you could let us know which area you are most interested in and why, we can make sure we won't disappoint you.
   >
   > It would also be helpful to know if there is any food you don't eat. This will make life easier for our cook.
   >
   > Looking forward to your reply.
   >
   > Best wishes
   >
   > Hillary Mason

   Write your reply to Hillary in 140–190 words in an appropriate style.

TEST YOURSELF

UNITS 3 & 4

VOCABULARY

1 Complete the sentences with the words in the list. There are four extra words.

best | accident | strict | grow | organised | well | private | bad-tempered
panic | soft | helmets | secret | row | imaginative

1. My parents were quite _____ when I was young. I couldn't do everything I wanted to do.
2. My mother was very _____. The house was always tidy with everything in the right place.
3. She always had our school things ready for us, even our cycling _____.
4. I had five brothers and although we were often very difficult, I don't think she was ever _____.
5. Both my parents did everything they could to help us do _____ in life.
6. They kept any arguments for when they were alone. They never argued in _____.
7. My dad invented great games for us. He really was very _____.
8. He was very calm. I never saw him in a _____.
9. Once we helped him prepare a surprise party for my mum. Everything had to be done in _____ so she wouldn't find out.
10. I think we were lucky to _____ up in such a family.

/10

GRAMMAR

2 Complete the sentences with the words in the list. There are two extra words.

few | enthusiasm | little | living | most | live | none | surprise

1. Josh doesn't like boxing much, so he went to the boxing match without much _____.
2. _____ of my friends could come to the party; they were all away on holiday.
3. When I was a child, I used to _____ in London.
4. Kyle has seen loads of films, but he's only read a _____ books.
5. Penny has never got used to _____ away from her family.
6. Samya wanted to spend a _____ more time on the photo selection for the project.

3 Find and correct the mistake in each sentence.

1. The test was such difficult that nobody got everything right.
2. Harry was used to be alone in the old house so he wasn't worried.
3. Sara was much scared to stay there after dark.
4. Manu listened with interesting to the interview with the local politician.
5. There was hardly any of space on the shelf, so I couldn't put the books there.
6. My grandmother always preferred her laptop. She never used to using a tablet.

/12

FUNCTIONAL LANGUAGE

4 Choose the correct options.

1. **A** I'll never / give up write a poem.
   B Don't be so / such pessimistic! I'm sure you can do it.
2. **A** But you're so / such a good writer. Can't you write one for me?
   B No chance / I can't do that – but I'll help.
3. **A** Oh, dear! This project is so / such difficult.
   B What's the problem? You're usually so / such an imaginative person.
4. **A** Oh! I'm give up / hopeless at drawing. This dog looks more like a bear!
   B Come on! Don't get so / such angry! Why don't you find a dog on the Internet and copy it?

/8

MY SCORE /30

22 – 30
10 – 21
0 – 9

47

PRONUNCIATION

UNIT 1
Diphthongs: alternative spellings

1 🔊 1.07 Read and listen to the five tongue twisters. Notice the different spellings of the same sounds.

1 **Si**mon **might**'ve **died** when he **climbed** on the **ice**.
2 **Joe** tip**toed** a**lone** through the **snow**.
3 We **stayed** until **late**; when it **rained** we went **straight** a**way**.
4 When they got **down** from the **mountain** they **found** it was just **out** of **town**.
5 The **boys** en**joyed** the **noise** as the water **boiled**.

2 🔊 1.08 Listen, repeat and practise.

UNIT 2
Phrasal verb stress

1 🔊 1.13 Read and listen to the dialogue below.

GILLIAN Moving to France when I was 9 was tough. It turned out all right though. I soon made new friends.
SAM How long did it take you to pick up French?
GILLIAN About three months. I hung out with my French friends every day, so that helped.
SAM Do you ever run into them now?
GILLIAN Run into them? I don't live in France any more!

2 Circle the correct words.

Red indicates ¹*primary / secondary* stress. Blue indicates ²*primary / secondary* stress. In two-part phrasal verbs, primary stress is usually on the ³*verb / particle* and secondary stress is on the ⁴*verb / particle*.

3 🔊 1.14 Listen, repeat and practise.

UNIT 3
Adding emphasis

1 🔊 1.18 Read and listen to the dialogue.

MILLIE Hannah's **such** a good tennis player! Did you see the match yesterday?
ROB Yes! It was **so** exciting!
MILLIE She didn't win, but she **did** play really well.
ROB It was **such** a pity she lost! She tried **so** hard.
MILLIE Yes, it was **such** a difficult match.
ROB I know. Anyway, I **do** think she's amazing!

2 🔊 1.18 Listen again. What is the effect of the words in **bold**?

3 🔊 1.19 Listen, repeat and practise.

UNIT 4
Pronouncing words with *gh*

1 🔊 1.23 Read and listen to the extracts from the 'Answers4U' web page. What do you notice about the pronunciation of *gh* in the words in bold?

PAUL At first I **thought** it wouldn't be a problem – but now I'm scared I'll only get **through** it with great difficulty.
SARAH Actually, the only box is the way we've been **brought** up to see problems. Try to stop seeing things as '**right**' or 'wrong'. If you try an idea and other people **laugh** at it, that's their problem, not yours. Anyway, **enough** from me. I hope these ideas help!

2 🔊 1.24 Listen, repeat and practise.

GET IT RIGHT!

UNIT 1
Verb patterns

> Learners often use the wrong verb form after certain verbs, using the gerund instead of *to* + infinitive and vice versa.
>
> ✓ *I'm looking forward to **going** to the festival.*
> ✗ *I'm looking forward ~~to go~~ to the festival.*

Which of these sentences are correct and which are incorrect? Rewrite the incorrect ones.

0 Ben was looking forward to climb the cliff.
   Ben was looking forward to climbing the cliff

1 They wanted going sailing but the weather conditions were too extreme.
   _____
   _____

2 I enjoy to wander around outdoor markets when I'm on holiday.
   _____
   _____

3 Jo refused to swing across the river on the rope.
   _____
   _____

4 Do you think you'll manage completing the mountain climb?
   _____
   _____

5 Tim doesn't mind helping out on the mountaineering course at weekends.
   _____
   _____

6 Kate had hoped reaching the glacier by early afternoon but slipped on the ice and broke her leg.
   _____
   _____

7 The children learnt building a shelter during the survival course.
   _____
   _____

8 Megan was thrilled when she got her exam results as she'd expected failing.
   _____
   _____

remember, *try*, *stop*, *regret* and *forget*

> Learners often use the wrong verb form after the verbs *remember*, *try*, *stop*, *regret* and *forget*, which can all be followed by both the gerund and infinitive but with different meanings.
>
> ✓ *I really think you should stop **smoking**.*
> ✗ *I really think you should ~~stop to smoke~~.*

Choose the correct verb form.

1 Did you remember *buying* / *to buy* some milk?
2 John stopped *getting a drink* / *to get a drink* at a café on the way to the beach.
3 I will never forget *climbing* / *to climb* Everest. It was the ultimate experience.
4 Kathryn tried *climbing* / *to climb* Everest three times but never succeeded.
5 Dan stopped *studying* / *to study* after the exam.
6 They regretted *going* / *to go* to the party as they didn't know anyone and they felt awkward.
7 Dad tried *completing* / *to complete* the crossword but it was impossible.
8 I regret *informing* / *to inform* you that there are no places left on the course.

UNIT 2
that and *which* in relative clauses

> Learners often use *that* instead of *which* in non-defining relative clauses.
>
> ✓ *Working leads to self-esteem, **which** is vital for most people.*
> ✗ *Working leads to self-esteem, ~~that~~ is vital for most people.*

Match the two parts of the sentences and rewrite them as one sentence using either *that* or *which*. Use *that* where possible.

0 The Arctic tern flies about 70,000 miles, — *b*
1 The grey whale is the animal —
2 Domenico Lucano had an idea —
3 Our teacher always praises us when we've done well in a test, —
4 I spoke to him using Italian, —
5 Elana has decided to live abroad, —

122

a helps give us confidence.
b is an amazing distance.
c swims about 18,000 km every year.
d I think is very brave of her.
e saved his village.
f I had learnt while working there.

0 *The Arctic tern flies about 70,000 miles, which is an amazing distance.*

Relative pronouns

> **Learners often omit relative pronouns in defining relative clauses when you can't.**
>
> ✓ I don't know the number of people **who** went to the festival.
> ✗ I don't know the number of ~~people went~~ to the festival.

Which of these sentences are correct and which are incorrect? Rewrite the incorrect ones.

0 Did you run into any of the people usually play there on Mondays?
   Did you run into any of the people who usually play there on Mondays?

1 The pedestrians crossing the road had to run to avoid being hit by the car.

2 There was a food shortage caused by the extreme weather last summer.

3 They went through a bad time lasted a few months.

4 Who is the man waving at us?

5 Those are the residents live in that building over there.

6 The Tuareg are the people regularly cross national borders.

UNIT 3
much vs. *many*

> **Learners often confuse *much* and *many*.**
>
> ✓ There are **many** more advantages than disadvantages.
> ✗ There are ~~much~~ more advantages than disadvantages.
>
> ✓ There was **much** more information on the website.
> ✗ There was ~~many~~ more information on the website.

Complete the sentences with *much* or *many*.

1 There wouldn't be so _____ naughty children if parents were stricter.
2 I can spend as _____ time as necessary making the costume.
3 She should ask Mrs Davies for advice. She knows so _____ about parenting.
4 The book contains _____ useful ideas about bringing up children.
5 You should come inside now. You've already spent too _____ time in the sun.
6 There is _____ more to be said about this but we don't have time now.

much and *most*

> **A common error for learners is mistakes with *most* by preceding it with *the* or following it by *of* when this isn't necessary.**
>
> ✓ **Most** drivers are careless.
> ✗ ~~The~~ most drivers are careless.
>
> ✓ **Most** parents find bringing up children a challenge.
> ✗ Most ~~of~~ parents find bringing up children a challenge.

Tick the correct sentences and cross the incorrect ones. Then rewrite the incorrect sentences correctly.

1 The most of my teachers at school were quite strict. ☐
2 Most of my friends use their phones a lot. ☐
3 James spent most of the time I was there getting ready for the fancy-dress party. ☐
4 Sally tried on a few outfits but the most of them were too big for her. ☐
5 It would be interesting to know if most of people agreed with Amy Chua's parenting ideas. ☐
6 Were the most of your old school friends at the reunion? ☐

UNIT 4
used to

> **Learners often make mistakes with *used to*, writing *use to* instead of *used to* and also using it to talk about present habits.**
>
> ✓ I **used** to help him when he was ill.
> ✗ I ~~use~~ to help him when he was ill.
>
> ✓ I **usually** go running twice a week if I have the time.
> ✗ I ~~use to~~ go running twice a week if I have the time.

Rewrite these incorrect sentences correctly.

1 Liam use to be very bad-tempered but he's nicer now.
2 There's a lot of planning involved in my job so I use to be organised.
3 When I was at school we use to sit in a row in some lessons.
4 They use to go to school by bus except for Tuesdays when they walk.
5 The man who use to live there moved to Spain.
6 Sarah used to watch a lot of TV when she hasn't got much homework.

WORKBOOK 4A   B2

Herbert Puchta, Jeff Stranks & Peter Lewis-Jones

CONTENTS

Welcome unit   4

UNIT 1 Survival	**10**
Grammar	10
Vocabulary	12
Reading	14
Writing	15
Listening	16
Exam practice: First	17

UNIT 2 Going places	**18**
Grammar	18
Vocabulary	20
Reading	22
Writing	23
Listening	24
Exam practice: First	25
Consolidation 1 & 2	**26**

UNIT 3 The next generation	**28**
Grammar	28
Vocabulary	30
Reading	32
Writing	33
Listening	34
Exam practice: First	35

UNIT 4 Thinking outside the box	**36**
Grammar	36
Vocabulary	38
Reading	40
Writing	41
Listening	42
Exam practice: First	43
Consolidation 3 & 4	**44**

Pronunciation   page 118   **Grammar reference**   page 122
Irregular verb list   page 128

WELCOME

A WHAT A STORY!
Descriptive verbs

1 Choose the correct options to complete the sentences.

1 The hurricane *demolished / fled / raged* everything in its path.
2 The prisoner *struck / smashed / dived* under the water to escape the bullets.
3 The family *smashed / fled / struck* from their burning home.
4 As she started to fall I managed to *grab / rage / scream* her by the arm.
5 The fire *demolished / raged / dived* through the trees.
6 The people *screamed / grabbed / demolished* in terror as the wave came towards them.
7 The robbers *smashed / flew / screamed* down a wall to break into the bank.
8 The car was *grabbed / dived / struck* by the falling tree.

Phrasal verbs

1 Complete the sentences with the correct form of the verbs in the list.

end | sort | stand | take
look | break | give | carry

1 I think I might _____ up yoga. It's really good for body and mind.
2 He studied medicine at university so I'm not sure how he _____ up as an accountant.
3 Can you believe it? Our car _____ down five miles from home.
4 I know I should _____ up eating so much chocolate but I think I'd find it too difficult.
5 They _____ on eating their picnic even though it started to rain.
6 When I have a problem my mum always helps me _____ it out.
7 I'm really _____ forward to the summer holidays. I need a rest.
8 Bill really _____ out in the class photo because he's so tall.

Elements of a story

1 Match the words with the definitions.

1 hero ☐
2 plot ☐
3 dialogue ☐
4 characters ☐
5 ending ☐
6 opening ☐
7 villain ☐
8 setting ☐

a the people in the story
b a bad man or woman
c how the story starts
d how the story finishes
e the man or woman in the story we identify with
f the place where the story happens
g what the people in the story say
h the storyline

2 Complete the text with the missing words.

So what do you need to write a successful story? Well to start with you need a good ¹_____ – without a great story you've got no chance. Of course any good story needs a selection of different ²_____, a ³_____ for the reader to identify with and a ⁴_____ to hate. And to help bring all these people alive you'll need to have good ⁵_____ between them. What they say and how they say it is so important. Then you'll need a ⁶_____ for your story. Where and when does the action happen? Is it the modern day, in the past or even in the future?

So now you've got all that, it's time to start writing. The ⁷_____ is essential. You'll need to get your reader's attention from the very beginning. And once you've got their attention hopefully they'll read right through so you'll need to give them a good ⁸_____ too, to make sure they won't feel they've wasted their time.

And that's all you need. That and a lot of luck.

Talking about past routines

1 🔊 02 **Listen and put the pictures in order.**

2 Complete the sentences so they are true for you.

1 When I was really young my mum/dad would
_____

2 My first teacher at school used to
_____

3 When I was upset I used to
_____

4 When it was my birthday, my parents would
_____

5 During the school holidays I would
_____

SUMMING UP

1 Put the dialogue in order.

	ANA	Well, for example, he'd tell a story about how a fire was raging through our house and how we needed to smash down the door. And he'd do all the actions.
1	ANA	My dad used to tell me really great stories when I was a kid.
	ANA	Yes it is. I really miss his stories.
	ANA	Really dramatic and exciting stories, and he would pretend they were happening to us.
	ANA	He was. I used to really look forward to his stories. But he gave up telling them as I got older.
	JAKE	That's a shame.
	JAKE	What kind of stories?
	JAKE	He sounds like a really fun dad.
	JAKE	What do you mean?

WELCOME

B AN UNCERTAIN FUTURE
Future plans

1 Match the sentence halves.

1 I don't leave ☐
2 You'll need to get a ☐
3 Many young people are waiting longer to start ☐
4 Before I start my career I'd love to travel ☐
5 I'd like to make enough money so I can ☐
6 My parents would love me to settle ☐

a a family these days.
b the world for a year or so.
c retire before I'm 60.
d down but I'm not ready yet.
e school for another two years.
f really good degree if you want to work for them.

Life plans

1 Put the events in the order that they happened.

☐ So I returned home and started doing a degree.

☐ So I decided to travel the world for a while until I made up my mind.

☐ When I was in Asia I suddenly realised what career I wanted to do – teaching.

☐ We started a family after I had been teaching for a few years.

[1] When I left school I wasn't too sure what I wanted to do.

☐ Next year I'm going to retire. I can't help wondering how it all passed so quickly.

☐ After the birth of my second son, I got promoted. I'm now a head teacher.

☐ In my final year of university I met the love of my life and we settled down.

Future continuous

1 Complete the sentences using the future continuous form of the verb in brackets.

Two months from now …

1 I _____ on a sunny beach in Greece. (lie)
2 I _____ exams anymore. (not do)
3 I _____ delicious food every night. (eat)
4 I _____ every morning at 6 am! (not get up)
5 I _____ in a 5-star hotel. (stay)
6 I _____ the bus to school every morning. (not take)

I can't wait for the summer holidays!

Being emphatic: so and such

1 Choose the correct option.

1 This exercise is *so / such* difficult.
2 Mr Peters is *so / such* a good teacher.
3 That was *so / such* a bad game of football.
4 I was *so / such* late for school today.
5 She gave me *so / such* a great present.
6 Andrew is *so / such* good at chess.
7 I feel *so / such* tired today.
8 We had *so / such* a good holiday.

2 Complete the sentences with *so* or *such*. Then match the sentences to the photos.

1 It's _____ a smart dog.
2 They're _____ a talented family.
3 I really am _____ tired.
4 It's _____ windy today.
5 They're _____ a bad team.
6 This cake is _____ delicious.

Extreme adjectives

1 Complete with the missing adjectives.

0 That film wasn't bad. It was t*errible*!
1 I don't find Maths interesting. I find it f_____!
2 That joke wasn't funny. It was h_____!
3 The water's not cold. It's f_____!
4 No, they weren't scared. They were t_____!
5 Their house isn't big. It's e_____!
6 That dog isn't small. It's t_____!
7 It isn't hot today. It's b_____!

2 Complete the second diary entry with extreme adjectives.

01/01/1996
Life's pretty good. I can't really complain. I live in a big house with my parents. We get on well most of the time. I like school. It's interesting and I really enjoy going most days. Mr Henderson, my Science teacher, is really funny. He makes me laugh and it's always fun in his lessons. In my spare time I go go-karting. It's a really exciting hobby. I won a trophy last week. It was pretty small but the size isn't important. It says 'Most Improved Driver' on it so I'm happy with it. I'm not sure my mum's so keen on my hobby. She's scared I'll have an accident. I tell her not to worry and that one day I'll be a world champion.

02/02/2016
Life's pretty ¹_____. I can't complain at all. I live in a ²_____ house with my wife and children. We get on well all of the time. I like my job. It's ³_____ and I really enjoy going most days. My boss is really ⁴_____. He makes me laugh and it's always fun hanging out with him. I'm a racing driver. It's a really ⁵_____ sport. I won a trophy last week. It was ⁶_____ but the size isn't important. It says 'World Champion' on it so I'm ⁷_____ with it. I'm not sure my mum's so keen on my job. She's ⁸_____ I'll have an accident. I tell her, 'Isn't it time you stopped worrying?'

SUMMING UP

1 Complete the dialogue with the words in the list. There are four extra words.

amazing | settle | terrible | promote
degree | enormous | so | such
retire | career | travel | huge

KATIE So what are your plans for the weekend, Conner?

CONNER Well my dad's going to ¹_____ from work next week so we're having an ²_____ party for him on Saturday. I mean it's going to be really big!

KATIE But he's ³_____ young!

CONNER I know, and the crazy thing is that the company offered to ⁴_____ him too.

KATIE So what made him decide to leave?

CONNER Well the money he got was ⁵_____ but it was ⁶_____ a stressful job.

KATIE Yes, money isn't everything.

CONNER Now he's got plans to ⁷_____ the world with Mum.

KATIE But what about you?

CONNER Well, I hope they're going to wait until I'm at university doing a ⁸_____. But the mood Dad's in, I can't be too sure!

C HOW PEOPLE BEHAVE

Personality

1 Complete the descriptions with adjectives.

1 He only thinks about himself and what's good for him. He's really s_____.
2 She always says 'please' or 'thank you'. She's very p_____.
3 You didn't need to buy me a present. That was very t_____ of you.
4 He never panics. He's a very c_____ person.
5 She's very l_____. She always seems to have so much energy.
6 He's very quiet, not because he's unfriendly, he's just a bit s_____.
7 He's very g_____ with both his money and, more importantly, his time.
8 He left without saying 'goodbye', which I thought was a bit r_____.

Using *should*

1 Write a reply. Use *should* or *shouldn't*.

0 'I'm really tired today.'
 You should have gone to bed earlier.
1 'It's Luis's birthday tomorrow.'
 _____
2 'I can't believe it. We've missed the bus.'
 _____
3 'My tooth is really hurting.'
 _____
4 'Mia's really upset with me.'
 _____
5 'I'm bored.'
 _____

2 Complete the dialogue with *should / shouldn't have* and the correct form of the verbs in the list.

stay | get up | bring | put | set

TEACHER Have you done your homework, Elsie?
ELSIE Umm, I have but I left it at home.
TEACHER But it was for today. You ¹_____ it with you.
ELSIE I know. I'm sorry but I was in such a hurry I left it on the kitchen table.
TEACHER You ²_____ earlier. Then you wouldn't have been in such a hurry.
ELSIE I know. I ³_____ my alarm clock but I forgot. And I ⁴_____ my book in my bag the night before. And I ⁵_____ up so late last night.

Career paths

1 Use the clues to complete the crossword and find the mystery profession.

1 They take all the rubbish from the roads.
2 My brother builds bridges and tunnels.
3 She tries to help people who find themselves in trouble with the police.
4 She looks after a 4-year-old and two 6-year-olds.
5 My aunt works in a really busy hospital in the middle of London.
6 He gets us to and from school.

2 Choose the correct option.

1 My aunt is a receptionist at the clinic. She works in *finance / healthcare*.
2 My whole family work in *public service / management*. Dad's a nurse, Mum's a teacher and my uncle is a policeman.
3 I'd like to work in *law / education*, maybe as a professor at a university.
4 If you want to get into medical school you'll need the right *qualifications / salary*.
5 There are more than 500 *employees / employers* working at the factory.
6 They're one of the biggest *employees / employers* in the region with more than 2,000 people working for them.
7 My mum's in *education / finance*. She's an accountant at the hospital.
8 I know he's in *law / healthcare*. He's a solicitor, I think.

Decisions

1 Match the sentence halves.

1 Come on, Alice. Make up ☐
2 Can you be quiet? I find it difficult to make ☐
3 It's an important decision. I need to think long ☐
4 Don't worry. You can always change ☐
5 It's been ten minutes already. Have you come ☐

a and hard about it.
b your mind later if you want to.
c your mind. Do you want a sandwich or not?
d to a decision yet?
e a decision when people are talking.

Permission

1 Choose the correct option.

1 Do your parents *allow / let / make* you do whatever you want?
2 I'm not *allowed / let / made* to go out on a school night.
3 My parents *let / make / allow* me do my homework before I can play on the tablet.
4 Our teacher *makes / lets / allows* us put up our hand if we want to ask a question.
5 My mum won't *allow / let / make* me come to your party.
6 Are we really *allowed / let / made* to go in that abandoned house?

2 Complete the sentences with the missing words.

1 Are you _____ to stay up late?
2 Does your teacher _____ you use phones in class?
3 Do your parents _____ you do your homework before you can watch TV?
4 Are you _____ to do any housework by your parents?
5 Do your parents _____ you to get up late at the weekends?
6 Do your teachers _____ you eat in class?

3 Write your answers to the questions in Exercise 2.

SUMMING UP

1 Put the dialogue in order.

	JIM	I hope you're right. Anyway, I'm allowed to use their family car.
1	JIM	Have you heard the news? I've got a summer job.
	JIM	I'm actually quite scared. I don't really have much experience with kids.
	JIM	I don't think I'm allowed to use it when I'm not working.
	JIM	Childminding for children from the same family every day.
	LUCY	Wow. You're very brave.
	LUCY	You'll be fine. You're kind and lively. That's all kids want.
	LUCY	You never know. You should ask them. A friend with a car! This is going to be a good summer.
	LUCY	Cool! Where are you going to take me?
	LUCY	Congratulations. What is it?

D NEW THINGS
Reporting verbs

1 Match each verb with a sentence.

invite ☐
recommend ☐
refuse ☐
explain [1]
agree ☐
demand ☐
persuade ☐
encourage ☐

1 To get to the station, you need to take the number 3 bus.
2 No, Bella, I won't take you to the party.
3 I want you to get out of my house, Ben. Now!
4 Would you like to go to the cinema, Jenny?
5 Come on, Jim. Come to the party with me. You will? Great!
6 You should enter the talent show. You're brilliant at singing, Lucy.
7 Read this book, Matt. You'll love it.
8 OK, Simon. I'll talk to your dad and see if I can change his mind.

2 Report the sentences in Exercise 1.

1 He *explained how to get to the station by bus.*
2 She _____
3 He _____
4 She _____
5 He _____
6 She _____
7 He _____
8 She _____

3 Complete with the reporting verbs in Exercise 1. There are three you won't use.

I can't believe I've ¹_____ to do a parachute jump with Tim. How did that happen? It all started when he ²_____ to me about this children's charity that he is involved with. I said it sounded interesting and he ³_____ me along to one of their meetings. So I went to see what it's all about. I didn't know they were organising a sponsored parachute jump. They asked me to get involved and of course I ⁴_____. I mean, I'm not mad. But they kept on trying to ⁵_____ me to do it and in the end I gave in and said 'yes'. And now I can't get out of it.

WELCOME

Negative adjectives

1 Rewrite the sentences using a negative adjective.

0 I'm not happy.
   I'm unhappy.

1 It's not true.
   _____

2 It's not a formal party.
   _____

3 They're not patient.
   _____

4 That wasn't responsible of you.
   _____

5 Buy it. It's not expensive.
   _____

6 They're not polite children.
   _____

7 I don't think that's possible.
   _____

Changes

1 Match the sentence halves.

1 If you're bored, why don't you take
2 The children are all doing
3 If children form
4 If he doesn't change his
5 Why's it so difficult to break
6 I'm not going to make
7 I'm finding French too hard. I might give
8 Sometimes I struggle

a any resolutions this new year.
b up having lessons.
c to understand maths. It can be so hard.
d bad habits?
e good habits when they're young, they'll never forget them.
f up a new hobby?
g ways, he's going to get into trouble one day.
h really well at their new school.

Regrets: *I wish … / If only …*

1 For each situation write two regrets: one about the present and one about the past.

0 I can't afford to buy my mum a birthday present.
   I wish I had more money.
   If only I hadn't spent all my money on clothes.

1 Sara refuses to speak to me.
   _____
   _____

2 I'm so tired I want to go to bed but I'm stuck here in my Science lesson.
   _____
   _____

3 All the popular boys are in the school football team.
   _____
   _____

4 I'm bored.
   _____
   _____

SUMMING UP

1 Complete the dialogue with the words/phrases in the list. There are four extra words/phrases.

encourage | struggle | wasn't | unhappy
am not | impossible | take up | gave up
demand | impolite | hadn't given it up | refuse

MARTHA What's up, Ben? You look a bit [1]_____.
BEN I'm OK. I'm just bored. I've got nothing to do.
MARTHA Why don't you [2]_____ a new hobby? That will fill your time.
BEN Like what?
MARTHA Guitar lessons. You've always wanted to play the guitar better.
BEN That's true. I wish I [3]_____ when I was a teenager. I'd be really good now.
MARTHA Well, it's not too late to start again.
BEN It is. It's [4]_____ for someone my age to start learning an instrument.
MARTHA What! You're 23!
BEN I know but I really [5]_____ with learning new things. I wish I [6]_____ that way but I am.
MARTHA OK then – be bored.
BEN What! That's not very nice.
MARTHA Well I'm trying to [7]_____ you but you [8]_____ to listen. I give up.
BEN I'm sorry, Martha. I'm just joking. And, you're right – it's never too late to start something new. In fact, I think I might just do that. Do you know any good teachers?
MARTHA That's more like it. In fact I do … My brother! He's great.

9

1 SURVIVAL

GRAMMAR
Verb patterns: to + infinitive or gerund SB page 14

1 ★☆☆ Write the verbs in the correct columns according to what they are followed by (to + infinitive or gerund).

~~keep~~ | suggest | manage | promise | ask
decide | detest | don't mind | miss | want
can't stand | enjoy | offer | choose

to + infinitive	gerund
	keep

2 ★★☆ Circle the correct form of the verbs to complete the mini-dialogues.

1 JANE Did Simon manage *to finish / finishing* his essay last night?
  HARRY Yes, so he's promised *coming / to come* climbing with us this weekend.
  JANE Fantastic. My dad's offered *to give / giving* us a lift to the climbing club.

2 KATE I suggested *to take / taking* a picnic but they don't want *to carry / carrying* it.
  SAM I don't mind *to carry / carrying* it.

3 ELIF Now I live in the city, I miss *to go / going* for long walks in the countryside.
  JO Really? I can't stand *to walk / walking* in the countryside.

4 ANNA You're very good at the violin!
  ZOE No, I'm not. I really enjoy *to play / playing* and I keep *to practise / practising* but I'm not getting any better.
  ANNA Ask Tom *to help / helping* you. He's a brilliant musician.

5 STEVE You'll never guess what? Tim came climbing with us.
  ELLIE But Tim detests *to climb / climbing*!

3 ★★☆ Complete the text with the correct form of the verbs in brackets.

I enjoy ¹_____ (climb) mountains, so last year, I decided ²_____ (climb) Ben Nevis in Scotland with a friend. We planned ³_____ (go) to Scotland in August, and we arranged ⁴_____ (stay) with a friend in Fort William for a few days. We started our climb at six am, and we hoped ⁵_____ (get back) down the mountain by two pm. The weather was good, so we managed ⁶_____ (reach) the summit in two hours. We never imagined ⁷_____ (see) such a beautiful view from the summit. The next day, we felt like ⁸_____ (climb) Ben Nevis again.

4 ★★★ Find five mistakes in the dialogue and correct them.

KATE I can't believe it. I managed climbing Devil's Rock this weekend.
MATT Did you? That's great.
KATE I've watched you climb it a couple of times but I never imagined to climb it myself. I'm hoping doing more climbing next weekend. I learnt descending the rock face using the rope. That was scary! What did you do at the weekend?
MATT I wanted coming climbing with you and the others but I had some homework to do.

5 ★★★ Complete the sentences so that they are true for you.

1 I enjoy _____
2 I started _____
3 I don't mind _____
4 I hate _____
5 I refuse _____
6 I love _____

10

1 SURVIVAL

Verbs + gerund and to + infinitive with different meanings SB page 15

6 ★☆☆ Match the sentences with their meanings.

1. I stopped to look at the view.
2. I stopped looking at the view.
3. He remembers buying a newspaper.
4. Remember to buy a newspaper, Tom.
5. He tried learning Chinese.
6. He tried to learn Chinese.
7. I'll never forget reading that article in the newspaper.
8. I forgot to read that article in the newspaper.

a. I'll always remember that article I read in the newspaper.
b. He knows he bought a newspaper.
c. I didn't remember to read that article in the newspaper.
d. He wasn't able to learn Chinese.
e. I didn't look at the view any more.
f. Don't forget to buy a newspaper.
g. I stopped so I could look at the view.
h. His goal was to impress his clients by speaking Chinese.

7 ★★☆ Complete the mini-dialogues with the correct form of the verbs in brackets.

1. A I forgot _____ (tell) you. We're going to London this weekend.
   B Lucky you!
2. A Did Helena finish her essay?
   B No, she didn't. She tried _____ (finish) it last night but she couldn't.
3. A I regret _____ (not leave) earlier on Saturday.
   B Yes, you missed the boat race.
4. A Do you still play the piano?
   B No, I stopped _____ (play) when I was nine.
5. A Do you remember _____ (lend) me JK Rowling's latest book?
   B Yes, I do. You haven't given it back yet.
6. A You left your guitar at Karen's house. Her mum rang me this morning.
   B Yes, I know. I stopped _____ (pick it up) on the way home just now.

8 ★★☆ Complete the sentences with the correct form of the verbs in the list.

eat | listen | tell | watch

1. I was revising for the History exam and then I stopped _____ to some music.
2. I listened to the first three songs and then I stopped _____ .
3. I remember _____ that film last year.
4. Remember _____ that film tonight. It's really good.
5. I've tried _____ more vegetables but I don't like them.
6. I tried _____ less but I still didn't lose any weight.
7. I regret _____ you that there aren't any more tickets for the concert.
8. I regret _____ Emma about the trip last weekend.

9 ★★★ Now write a true sentence for each of the situations. Think of …

1. something you regret doing or saying.
   _____
2. something you remember doing or saying when you were in primary school.
   _____
3. something you've tried doing.
   _____
4. something you've stopped doing.
   _____
5. something you forgot to do recently.
   _____

GET IT RIGHT! 👁

to or gerund after certain verbs

Learners often omit *to* or the gerund after certain verbs.

✓ We decided **to** go out for a meal.
✗ We ~~decided go~~ out for a meal.

Correct the errors in the sentences.

1. Jenny couldn't afford do the survival course.
   _____
2. He started feel a bit awkward as no one was talking to him.
   _____
3. Ethan suggested have an early night before the exam.
   _____
4. I never promised help you with your homework!
   _____
5. Do they practise to sing every evening?
   _____
6. We wanted leave right away but we couldn't.
   _____

VOCABULARY

Word list

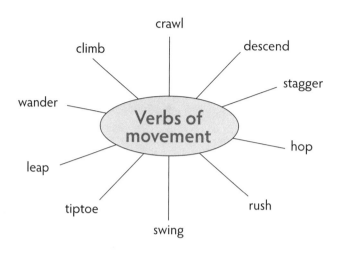

Verbs of movement: crawl, climb, descend, stagger, wander, hop, leap, rush, tiptoe, swing

Adjectives to describe uncomfortable feelings

puzzled
stuck
desperate

ashamed
guilty
awkward

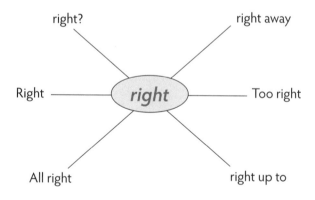

right: right?, right away, Right, Too right, All right, right up to

Key words in context

commercially	I don't think your product will be **commercially** successful. You won't have very many sales.
extreme	The weather conditions were **extreme**. It was very unusual to see such a snowstorm.
knot	He tied a **knot** at the end of the rope.
risky	It was **risky** to climb down the rock face without a safety rope but they had to do it.
shelter	It was snowing hard. We had to build a **shelter** to protect us from the snow and the cold.
slip	I **slipped** on the ice and fell over backwards.
stunt	That was a dangerous **stunt**. He jumped over three buses on a motorbike.
thrilled	I was **thrilled** when I won the race. My mum and dad were very happy too.
ultimate	Climbing Ben Nevis was the **ultimate** challenge for Jake. He had trained for months.

1 Survival

Verbs of movement SB page 14

1 ★☆☆ Find ten verbs of movement.

O	C	L	I	M	B	T	T	T	H	P
D	S	S	A	Y	N	I	E	C	A	H
N	W	C	A	T	B	P	L	E	T	R
E	I	W	R	R	K	T	L	A	G	E
C	N	S	E	A	L	O	P	W	L	G
S	G	M	E	E	W	E	S	O	E	G
E	H	R	U	S	H	L	I	N	H	A
D	W	A	N	D	E	R	T	D	E	T
B	R	E	A	T	H	L	E	G	R	S

2 ★★☆ Complete the text about the race with the past tense of the verbs of movement in Exercise 1. There are two you won't use.

Jake ⁰ _crawled_ through the tunnel on his hands and knees. Then he held onto the rope and ¹_____ across the river. He ²_____ very quietly past the house on the other side of the river. Then he quickly ³_____ up the mountain. In thick fog, he slowly ⁴_____ down the other side of the mountain. After that, he ⁵_____ across the flat ground. He was in a hurry to finish now. Then suddenly, he fell and hurt his left leg, so he ⁶_____ on his right leg to the finish line. Everybody cheered. He ⁷_____ through the crowds of people and he shook hands with all his fans.

Adjectives to describe uncomfortable feelings SB page 16

3 ★★☆ Read the situations. How would you feel? Choose one of the adjectives.

1 You don't know the answer to the next question on the exam paper. You can't do the next question until you've completed this one.
   You are *stuck / puzzled*.

2 Last night you ate your brother's chocolate bar. He doesn't know yet.
   You feel *guilty / desperate*.

3 You are at a party. Everybody knows each other but you don't know anybody.
   You feel *awkward / puzzled*.

4 You put your house keys on the desk. Now they aren't there.
   You are *ashamed / puzzled*.

5 You shouted at one of your friends yesterday.
   You feel *ashamed / guilty* of yourself.

6 You are locked in a room in a castle. You have no phone and there is no food. Nobody knows you are there.
   You feel *desperate / stuck*.

4 ★★★ Write a new situation for each feeling.

1 (puzzled) _____

2 (stuck) _____

3 (desperate) _____

4 (ashamed) _____

5 (guilty) _____

6 (awkward) _____

WordWise SB page 19
right

5 ★★☆ Complete the mini-dialogues with the phrases in the list.

right | right away | Too right
right up to | All right | Right

1 **A** Karen's just emailed me about the concert on Saturday. Do we want tickets?
   B Of course we do.
   A I'll email her back _____ then.

2 **A** Did you guess who the thief was?
   B No, I didn't know _____ the end of the book.

3 **A** Did you remember to buy the tickets?
   B I didn't buy them in the end. They were £50 a ticket. That's too expensive.
   A _____ . I don't want to pay that much for a ticket either.

4 **A** Sorry, I'll just answer the phone.
   B Go ahead.
   [later]
   A Sorry about that. It was James. _____ . What were we talking about?

5 **A** Can I come with you and Sam to the match on Saturday?
   B Yes, of course.
   A You're setting off early, _____ ?
   B Yes, we're leaving at 8 o'clock.

6 **A** Can I borrow your ruler?
   B _____ . But don't forget to give me it back.

READING

1 REMEMBER AND CHECK Answer these questions. Then check your answers on page 13 in the Student's Book.

1. Why did Simon and Joe decide to take the more dangerous route down the Siula Grande?
2. Why did the trip take longer than they had expected?
3. What did Joe break?
4. Why did Simon decide to leave his friend, Joe?
5. How long did it take Joe to descend the rest of the mountain?
6. Who saved Joe's life?

2 Read the article quickly and answer the questions.

1. Which body parts need to be very strong to free climb?
2. What is the importance of these numbers: 914, 19 and 27?

A Story of Teamwork and Perseverance

How do you climb a smooth rock face? In 2015, two young American climbers showed us how. Tommy Caldwell and Kevin Jorgeson became the first free climbers to climb the Dawn Wall of the El Capitan rock formation in California.

Free climbers don't use ropes when they climb. They only use their hands and feet. However, they do have ropes to hold them if they fall.

El Capitan is 914m high. That's almost 100m higher than the world's tallest building, the Burj Khalifa tower in Dubai, which is 163 floors high. The climb took Caldwell and Jorgeson 19 days. They ate, drank and slept in small tents hanging from the rock face. They even read books there! They brewed coffee on special hanging stoves. Every few days, a friend on the ground climbed up on a rope and brought them new supplies of food and water.

So how do you climb a smooth rock face? A lot of it relies on the strength of your fingertips. The climbers needed to stop and rest some days so that their fingertips could heal. To make their cuts heal quicker they used superglue and tape.

Unlike expeditions of a hundred years ago, people around the world could watch every moment of this climb as it happened. In their breaks, the climbers updated their social media accounts and spoke to journalists on the phone. A photographer and good friend, also hanging off the wall, captured every move on film and uploaded the photos on Instagram for people all around the world to see. 'Inspirational' – 'What a remarkable achievement! I'm awed.' – 'Awesome! Amazing! And a true friendship!' – 'What bravery and courage!' These are just some of the comments people tweeted as they watched the amazing climb.

A lot of the climbing was at night and they chose to climb in the middle of winter. Why was that? Well, fingertips sweat less in cooler temperatures and the rubber on shoes can grip better. They began their climb on the 27th December 2014 and they planned to live on the wall until they reached the top. They promised not to return to the ground during their climb.

Caldwell was the stronger and more experienced climber, and he was always ahead of Jorgeson. For ten days, Jorgeson continued to fall during his daily climbs. He knew that he was delaying his friend. But this climb was about teamwork and friendship. 'More than anything, I want to get to the top together,' said Caldwell on day 13. He couldn't imagine finishing without his friend. Finally on day 19 the two climbers made it to the top.

3 Read the article again and mark the sentences T (true) or F (false).

1. Caldwell and Jorgeson were the first free climbers to manage to climb the wall.
2. El Capitan is in a national park in New Mexico.
3. El Capitan is a few metres shorter than the world's tallest building.
4. People all around the world were able to see pictures of the climb on social media.
5. The climbers' shoes grip better in warmer temperatures.
6. They started to climb the Dawn Wall in January 2015.
7. The two climbers decided not to descend to the ground until they had successfully reached the top of the Dawn Wall.
8. Caldwell wanted to finish the climb before his friend, Jorgeson.

4 Many people tweeted as they watched the amazing climb. What comment would you make?

Pronunciation
Dipthongs: alternative spellings
Go to page 118.

DEVELOPING WRITING

A travel advertisement: review for an adventure holiday

1 Read Miriam's review. What do you notice about the style of writing?

a It is formal. ☐
b It is informal. ☐

2 What does Miriam use in her review?

a She uses some questions. ☐
b She uses very long sentences. ☐

My Climb to Confidence

What's 4,167 metres high, in Morocco and a challenge to climb? Mount Toubkal of course! Mount Toubkal is North Africa's highest mountain. And guess what? I managed to climb it this autumn. Yes, I actually climbed to the summit of a mountain.

The climb was a fantastic experience. The trekking was tough though, especially on the final day. We walked for twelve hours, and on the other three days we walked for eight or nine hours. I was exhausted when we finally reached the camp each evening. It was a four-day trek and we spent three icy cold nights camping. I went with my mum and dad and my older brother, who's nineteen. The climb was challenging for all of us. Each day, we stopped to have a picnic lunch, and the views were spectacular. I really regret not taking a camera. The rest of the holiday was fun too, but the climb up Mount Toubkal was the highlight for me. I think the whole trip was character building and I definitely feel more confident now I've done it.

Any tips? Yes. Remember to take a hat. The sun is fierce. Don't forget to take a water bottle with you and some water purification tablets. Prepare for a challenging walk.

3 Answer the questions.

1 How does Miriam describe Mount Toubkal?

2 How did Miriam feel when she reached the camp each evening?

3 Who did Miriam go with?

4 How did Miriam feel after the trip?

5 What tips does Miriam give?

4 Read the review again and find the adjectives. What do they describe? Write the nouns/pronouns. Then look in a thesaurus and find another adjective you could use instead.

Adjective	Noun	My new choice of adjective
1 tough	trekking	
2 exhausted		
3 icy cold		
4 challenging		
5 spectacular		
6 fierce		

5 Write a review for an adventure holiday. It can be for a holiday you have been on or a made up holiday. Write 200–250 words.

CHECKLIST ✓

☐ Use informal language
☐ Include interesting adjectives
☐ Use verbs of movement
☐ Include an introductory paragraph, main body, conclusion and travel tips

LISTENING

1 🔊04 Read the sentences below. Then listen and write the numbers of the dialogues, 1, 2 or 3 in the boxes.

1 They are in the middle of a challenge. One of them wants to give up. ☐

2 They have climbed a high mountain and they want a new challenge. ☐

3 They watch a video about people running, climbing, jumping and swinging over walls and buildings. ☐

2 🔊04 Listen again and complete the sentences with one word.

1 Sammy wants James to come and watch a _____.
2 Parkour started in _____.
3 Chris can't continue because he can't crawl through the _____.
4 The weather's very bad. It's just started to _____.
5 Jake enjoys going to the climbing club because everyone is very _____.
6 The climb up Ben Nevis was a _____ for Jake.

DIALOGUE

1 Complete these parts of the dialogues with the phrases in the list.

Of course you can | that's too easy | I bet you | I think you're probably right | I'll never manage to | I bet you | I challenge you | No problem

1 SAMMY Wow! Did you see that? _____ can't do that.
  JAMES _____ can.
  SAMMY All right. _____ to jump onto the kitchen table.
  JAMES But _____.
  SAMMY Yes, easy and safe. You need proper training to do Parkour.

2 CHRIS You go on ahead, Susie. _____ crawl through that tunnel.
  SUSIE _____, Chris. Come on. Keep going. You're doing really well. I bet you can crawl through that tunnel faster than I can.

3 JAKE It was a challenge but I'm glad I've done it.
  LOUISE Same here. What's our next challenge? I bet we can climb Mount Everest one day.
  JAKE _____. It won't be for a few years though. I don't think we're ready for that yet.
  LOUISE _____. We need a bit more practice before we take on that challenge. Now, where were we? … I know. You were showing me how to do that knot.

PHRASES FOR FLUENCY **SB page 19**

1 Match the two halves of the phrases.

1 Same   ☐   a a shout
2 Something   ☐   b what?
3 Give me   ☐   c deal
4 You know   ☐   d were we?
5 Where   ☐   e here
6 It's a   ☐   f or other

2 Complete the dialogues with phrases from Exercise 1.

1 A Come along to the indoor climbing club and I'll teach you. I'm a trainer there.
  B _____ When do I start?

2 A Dinner's not ready yet.
  B OK. _____ when it's ready.

3 A Rob's going on an adventure holiday this September. It's a trek across the desert in Jordan.
  B I know. I thought he was crazy at first. But _____ Now I think I want to go with him. It's a real challenge.

4 A Sorry about that, Matt. I had to answer a call. Now, _____
  B You were just showing me the route for Saturday's trek.
  A Ah, yes.

5 A I'm sorry I haven't called you this week. I've had a lot of things to do.
  B _____ I've been really busy with the band.

6 A Have you seen Kate recently?
  B No. She's at football training or tennis club or _____.

CAMBRIDGE ENGLISH: First

Reading and Use of English Part 4

1 For questions 1–5, complete the second sentence so that it has a similar meaning to the first sentence, using the word given. Do not change the word given. You must use between two and five words, including the word given. Here is an example (0).

Example:

0   I moved here five years ago.
    FOR
    I _'ve lived here for five_ years.

1   I would rather not see that film.
    PREFER
    I _____ that film.

2   I won't leave him there alone.
    REFUSE
    I _____ there alone.

3   I can't afford to buy this laptop.
    ENOUGH
    I _____ money to buy this laptop.

4   She wasn't able to complete her homework last night.
    MANAGE
    She _____ her homework last night.

5   I remember my first swimming lesson.
    FORGET
    I _____ first swimming lesson.

> ### Exam guide: key word transformation
>
> In this part of the exam, there are six questions. Each has a complete sentence and a second gapped sentence. You must complete the second sentence with two to five words so that it means the same as the first sentence. There is a key word which you must include.
> - Remember contractions count as two words.
> - You should always give every question a try. It's possible to get a point for one correct word.
> - Train yourself to think of different ways of saying things.

2 For questions 1–6, complete the second sentence so that it has a similar meaning to the first sentence, using the word given. Do not change the word given. You must use between two and five words, including the word given. Here is an example (0).

Example:

0   My mum didn't let me go to the cinema last night.
    ALLOW
    My mum _didn't allow me to_ go to the cinema last night.

1   It's been months since I last went swimming.
    BEEN
    I _____ several months.

2   We haven't got enough time to go and see the art exhibition.
    TOO
    It's _____ and see the art exhibition.

3   I couldn't see the play last night.
    ABLE TO
    I _____ the play last night.

4   Nobody has managed to climb that rock face yet.
    SUCCEEDED
    Nobody _____ that rock face yet.

5   I stopped so I could buy a newspaper.
    TO
    I _____ a newspaper.

6   I'd like to have a bath.
    FEEL
    I _____ a bath.

2 GOING PLACES

GRAMMAR
Relative clauses (review) [SB page 22]

1 ★★ Complete the gaps with *who*, *which* or *that* and put D (defining) or ND (non-defining).

0 People __who__ move to a big city can find it hard to meet people. [D]
1 My sister Jane, _____ lives in New York, has made a lot of friends there.
2 The café, _____ opened near the university, is a good place to meet people.
3 Paul, _____ has just moved in next door to me, has four sisters.
4 It's not always easy to meet people _____ like the same things as you.
5 Of the six flats, the one _____ Sally shares with four friends is the smallest.

2 ★★ Find and correct the mistakes in each sentence.

0 I'm very proud of my mother who works for a local charity.
   I'm very proud of my mother, who works for a local charity.
1 This is a photograph who I took in Italy.
2 The boy which bought my bike lives in this street.
3 My mother who is a doctor often has to work at weekends.
4 I've got a new phone who is far better than my old one.
5 The player, who scored the winning goal in the 2014 World Cup final, was Mario Götze.
6 I don't really like people, who talk a lot.

which to refer to a whole clause [SB page 22]

3 ★★ Write sentences from the prompts, using *which*.

0 Some people / listen / to very loud music / can / damage / their ears
   Some people listen to very loud music, which can damage their ears.
1 My father / walks / to work / is / good / for his health
2 My grandfather / has / three large dogs / means / he / gets / plenty of exercise
3 Some blind people / have / guide dogs / gives / them more independence
4 My sister / spends / hours / working / on the computer / sometimes / gives / her / a headache

4 ★★ Find pairs of ideas. Then write sentences using *which*. Make any other necessary changes.

0 ~~bus to school / cost £2.50~~
1 I like / watch films at home
2 friend / going / live in Colombia
3 mother's car / stolen last week
4 famous band / play in our town next week

a be / big change in lifestyle
b ~~be / very expensive for me~~
c not happen / very often
d mean / take bus to work
e be / cheaper / go / cinema

0 *The bus to school costs £2.50, which is very expensive for me.*
1
2
3
4

2 GOING PLACES

Omitting relative pronouns and reduced relative clauses SB page 25

5 ★☆☆ **Complete the gaps with *that / which / who* or – if the pronoun is not necessary.**

1 Patrick paid back the money _____ he owed me last week.
2 I know a lot of people _____ have eaten at that restaurant.
3 There are a few things _____ I want to keep with me.
4 This is the book _____ Mimi gave me for my birthday.
5 These aren't the photos _____ were in the newspaper.
6 I'm the sort of person _____ likes to spend time alone.

6 ★★☆ **Complete the dialogue with *who / which / that* or – if the pronoun is not necessary.**

JANET Greg, you've moved a lot. What are the things ¹_____ you think are important about moving?

GREG Yes, well, I think the thing ²_____ is most important is to be optimistic about the move. Of course there are things ³_____ you'll miss, but think of all the exciting things there will be. New places, new people!

JANET But what about my friends? This is the only place ⁴_____ I've ever lived in!

GREG You can keep in touch with the people ⁵_____ are your most important friends. And you can visit – you're going to live in Ireland, right? Not on the moon!

JANET I know, but you need to take a train and then the ferry, ⁶_____ makes it complicated and expensive. And what if I don't make new friends?

GREG Look, don't worry! You're an outgoing person ⁷_____ makes friends quickly – you'll be OK. But you know, one thing ⁸_____ I like to do before I move is make a scrapbook ⁹_____ will remind me of the place and the people. I put photos, names, birthdays and email addresses in it, ¹⁰_____ helps me to keep in touch with the friends ¹¹_____ I made.

JANET That's a great idea! Thanks, Greg.

7 ★★☆ **Join the sentences to make one sentence.**

0 Catarina is an Italian student. She is studying English in London.
Catarina is an Italian student studying English in London.

1 Walter fell and hurt himself. He was painting a wall.
_____

2 We gave a lift to two students. They were trying to get to London.
_____

3 I met a French guy on the train. He was going to the same place as me.
_____

4 A scientist accidentally discovered Post-It notes. He was trying to invent a strong glue.
_____

5 The crew of the ship found a man. He was hiding in the lifeboat.
_____

GET IT RIGHT! 👁
which and who

A common error for learners is to use *which* instead of *who* or vice versa in relative clauses.

✓ *I met some friendly people **who** became friends of mine.*
✗ *I met some friendly people **which** became friends of mine.*

Complete the sentences with *which* or *who*.

1 Please let me know _____ is the most direct way to the conference.
2 Most of the immigrants _____ moved to the village found work.
3 The motorists _____ use this road are kindly asked to drive more slowly.
4 There are a lot of people moving to this area, _____ means there will be fewer parking places.
5 Sam had a year out in Italy, _____ is a beautiful country.
6 Lucy turned out to be someone _____ you can rely on.
7 The Aborigines, _____ have been living there for 40,000 years, have few possessions.
8 The boat _____ the refugees were sailing on arrived safely in the port.

VOCABULARY

Word list

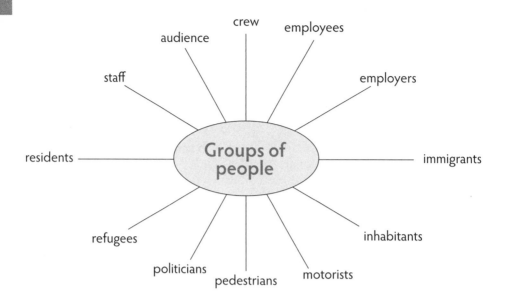

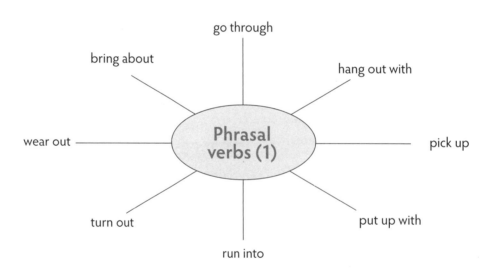

Key words in context

abroad	I don't live in my own country anymore – I live **abroad**.
compassion	She's had a very bad time recently – we need to show her some **compassion**.
courage	I've never sung in front of other people – I don't have the **courage**.
desperately	They've got no money at all – they're **desperately** poor.
homesickness	After two months away from home, my **homesickness** started to get better.
invaluable	I would never have succeeded without your help – it was **invaluable**.
mayor	In our city, we choose a new **mayor** every four years.
overall	We had a few days of rain, but mostly it was sunny, so **overall** the summer's been good.
praise	He told the truth and people **praised** him for his honesty.
renovate	My house is old now, so I'm going to **renovate** it.
severe	Sometimes the temperature is -25° – the winter can be really **severe**.
shortage	It hasn't rained for six months, so now we've got a water **shortage**.

2 GOING PLACES

Groups of people SB page 22

1 ★★ Complete the crossword.

1. The factory is the town's biggest …
2. It's a really big company – there are more than a thousand … there.
3. You can't drive here – this is a … zone.
4. Big, noisy lorries use this street, and some … are unhappy about it.
5. It's a huge city – there are about twelve million … here.
6. There is a large population of North African … in our town.
7. The plane was carrying 90 passengers and seven … members.
8. The accident was caused by a … who was driving too fast.
9. There are more than 30 teachers on the … of the school.
10. A lot of people in the … didn't like the film, and started to leave.
11. She escaped from her country and now she's a …
12. She's an important … and hopes to become the leader of her party soon.

Pronunciation
Phrasal verb stress
Go to page 118.

2 ★★ Which people might say these things? (There may be more than one possibility.)

1. Cyclists – they're terrible, I can't stand them.
2. The boss is OK but she makes us work really hard too!
3. I promise that we will make this country better.
4. It isn't always easy to make a new start in another country.
5. Speak up! We can't hear you here at the back.
6. We really love living here – it's great.

Phrasal verbs (1) SB page 24

3 ★ Circle the correct options.

1. I thought the exam would be difficult, but it *turned out / brought about* to be easy.
2. He's horrible – why do you *hang out with / run into* him?
3. The neighbours are so noisy – I can't *go through / put up with* it any more.
4. We complained so much that we *brought about / picked up* some changes.
5. I don't really speak Japanese – I just *picked up / put up with* some phrases.
6. Isn't it funny when you *run into / hang out with* someone you haven't seen for ages?
7. I worked really hard on Monday – I was *turned out / worn out*.
8. Don't worry – it's just a bad time I'm *wearing out / going through*.

4 ★★ Complete each sentence with one or two words.

1. Yesterday I ran _____ an old friend of my mother's.
2. They walk so quickly that they wear me _____!
3. Everyone said it was going to rain, but it turned _____ to be a lovely day.
4. I'm going to hang _____ my friends this afternoon.
5. Be nice to her – she's going _____ a bad time right now.
6. He's never had French lessons – he just picked it _____ in France.
7. We hope these changes will bring _____ some better results.
8. You're horrible! I don't know why I put _____ you!

READING

1 **REMEMBER AND CHECK** Match the phrases from columns A, B and C. Then check your answers in the text on page 21 of the Student's Book.

A	B	C
1 Many young people	started an organisation	to house the refugees.
2 Domenico Lucano	went and visited Riace	because there weren't enough jobs.
3 Lucano	had to work	called Città Futura.
4 The refugees	saw some people on the beach	to get ideas for their towns and cities.
5 Lucano	used empty buildings	who had escaped their own country.
6 The male refugees	which meant that	so they could be rented to tourists.
7 There are more children,	left Riace	to earn their food and accommodation.
8 Other politicians	renovated houses	the school could reopen.

2 Read the blog. How does the writer usually feel about getting lost? How did she feel at the end of this story?

The joys of getting lost

Most of us like to know where we are and where we're going. It can feel strange to be lost – sometimes very uncomfortable, too. The words 'being lost' make us think of a dark wood, or a dark city street: threatening and scary. But that's not always the case.

When I was about twelve, we were on holiday in Venice. My dad's a really keen photographer and he said that he was going to get up the following morning at 5 o'clock and go out to take photos as the sun came up. Mum wasn't interested, but I said I'd go with him. (Of course, that was only because he promised I could have the biggest ever bowl of Italian ice cream if I did! Why else would I get up at 5 in the morning?!)

So at 5 am we left the hotel and started walking. There was almost no one in the streets, which is pretty rare in Venice.

As the sun began to come up, Dad started taking photographs and I just looked around. Every time he walked off, I followed him, down small streets and over little bridges.

After about an hour and a half, I turned to him. 'Dad,' I asked, 'where are we?' He looked at me and said, 'You know, I have no idea.' I immediately felt a bit scared, but Dad just smiled and laughed. 'We're lost!' he said. I told him to get out his map or phone. He looked at me. 'Map? Phone? I only brought the camera. Come on, let's get more lost!' And he laughed again.

His laughter relaxed me and made me feel safe. We started to walk again. People were appearing on the streets – shops and cafés began to open, and as the sun came up the narrow streets started to fill with light, to Dad's delight.

I began to forget that we were lost, and just started watching and taking in everything that was happening around me. We stopped and had a sandwich for breakfast – Dad's terrible Italian was just enough for us to get what we wanted, even in a place away from the tourist track.

Finally, after about four hours of wandering around, Dad said: 'Hey! This is our street!' And we were back. Mum was in the breakfast room of the hotel when we came in. 'Where have you been?' she asked, anxiously. 'We got lost!' I said with a huge grin.

These days we have so many things to stop us from getting lost – maps, GPS, apps on our phones, and so on. But Dad showed me that being lost can sometimes simply be something to enjoy.

3 Read the blog again. Mark the sentences T (true), F (false) or DS (doesn't say).

1 When people think of 'being lost', they sometimes feel scared.
2 The writer's father is a professional photographer.
3 The streets in Venice are often empty.
4 The writer's father never took his phone with him when he took photographs.
5 The writer's father spoke good Italian.
6 They had breakfast in a place where tourists often went.
7 The writer's mother was worried about them.
8 The writer now gets lost quite often, in order to have adventures.

4 Write a short paragraph (50–80 words) to say how you feel about getting lost. Give an example of a time it happened to you.

2 GOING PLACES

DEVELOPING WRITING

Writing a letter to a friend

1 Read Marcos's letter to Jodie.

1 Where is he?
2 What difficulties does he talk about?

> Hi Jodie,
> How's everything with you in England? ¹Sorry I haven't written before but there's just been so much to do since I left Brazil to come here.
>   And now here I am in Vancouver, on my year exchange! You know that I'm staying with a family here, right? They're the Johnsons, who live in an area called Oakridge: it's a few kilometres from the city centre but there are buses and a train, so ²easy to get there. The Johnsons are very friendly and they've helped me settle in. They haven't got any kids but I've made some friends my age round here, and I go to the language course three mornings a week and I've got friends there too.
>   Talking of language – well, that's been the tricky thing, especially listening. People don't talk like in the books at school! I mean, ³no problem when I'm talking to one person, but in a big group, it can be hard to follow the conversation. Still, it's getting easier!
>   Otherwise, ⁴all good. I thought a lot of things would be very different here, but they aren't. One thing, though, is you have to remember to leave a tip in restaurants. ⁵Not like in Brazil, where the tip's always added to the bill. And when you buy something, you have to remember that they add tax at the check-out so you always pay more than what's on the label!
>   OK, ⁶got to go. Write and tell me how you are.
> Marcos

2 In each of the underlined parts of the letter, Marcos left something out before the underlined word(s). Match these phrases to the underlined parts 1–6.

a there's ☐   b I'm ☐   c it's ☐   d It's ☐   e I've ☐   f it's ☐

Writing tip

- We often leave certain words out in informal speaking and writing (it's called *ellipsis*). It is usually the subject and the auxiliary verb that are left out, for example:
Did you have a nice weekend? becomes *Have a nice weekend?* (leaving out the subject 'you' and the auxiliary 'did')

3 What could be left out from these sentences? Rewrite the sentences.

0 It's good to see you.
Good to see you.

1 There are no worries, we can do this easily.

2 Are you having a good time?

3 Do you see what I mean?

4 Imagine that you are doing an exchange programme in an English-speaking country. Write a letter to a friend about your experience. Write 200–250 words.

Include:
- which country you are in
- who you are staying with
- what difficulties you've had with language
- any cultural differences you've had to adjust to.

CHECKLIST ✓

☐ Use a style of an informal letter
☐ Use at least two examples of ellipsis
☐ Mention language and cultural difference
☐ Write 200–250 words

LISTENING

1 🔊 06 Listen to two conversations. Complete each sentence with between 1 and 3 words.

CONVERSATION 1

1 Jill has won a _____ a magazine.
2 The prize is a _____ day trip to South Africa.
3 She won't have to _____ on the trip.
4 Max wants to know how many people _____ is for.

CONVERSATION 2

5 Monika and Graham are looking at _____ comic books.
6 Monika's grandfather collects _____.
7 He started his collection when he was _____ as a young man.
8 _____ the money in his collection is old.

2 🔊 06 Listen again. Complete these parts of the conversations with 1 or 2 words.

CONVERSATION 1

JILL Well, in ¹_____, I entered it. I kind of thought I knew lots of the answers, most of them in fact. And so I thought 'OK, why not?'

MAX And …? Hold on, you're not telling me …

JILL Yes. I won! I heard today. The magazine phoned me up and told me I'd won.

MAX That's ²_____! Wow. Well done. So – you've got a free trip to South Africa?

JILL That's right. I can ³_____ it myself.

CONVERSATION 2

GRAHAM Do you collect anything, Monika?

MONIKA No – but my grandfather's got ⁴_____ collection of money from all over the world. I think he's got coins and notes from ⁵_____ a hundred different countries.

GRAHAM That's ⁶_____ collection!

DIALOGUE

1 Put the dialogues in order.

1

☐ A Go on – surprise me.
[1] A I hear you're going to Scotland for the weekend.
☐ A That's incredible.
☐ B Well, I got a return ticket for £57.50.
☐ B I know. It's amazing, isn't it? I could hardly believe it myself.
☐ B Yes, by train. I bought a really cheap ticket online last night. You'll never believe what I paid.

2

☐ A Pretty interesting, I thought. You know, they move around with camels, and they can travel up to sixty kilometres a day.
☐ A Did you see the documentary last night about the Tuareg?
☐ A I know. And in that kind of heat. It's almost unbelievable.
☐ B No, I missed it. Was it any good?
☐ B I'm not sure I'd want to do it, I have to say.
☐ B Wow. That's quite a distance.

3

☐ A In Alaska. And it's winter there. He wrote me an email – he said that sometimes, it's -25 degrees.
☐ A My friend Pete's gone travelling around the world.
☐ A I know. How do people survive in temperatures like that?
☐ B Really? I knew it got cold there, but not that cold!
☐ B I've got a better question. Why on earth did Pete choose to go somewhere so cold!?
☐ B Oh, right. So where is he now?

2 Write two dialogues of six lines each. Choose from these situations. Look back at Exercise 1 to help you.

1 Two friends are talking. One of them watched a football match. A player scored five goals.
2 Two friends are talking. One of them did an online quiz and got 49/50.
3 Two friends are talking. One of them has a new friend who is 2.12 metres tall.
4 Two friends are talking. One of them is saving to buy a musical instrument. It's very expensive.

CAMBRIDGE ENGLISH: First

Writing part 2: an article

Exam guide: writing an article

In part 2 of the writing exam you are asked to write a text from a choice of text types in about 140–190 words. This will sometimes be an article, for example, for a school magazine or a teen website.

Remember that the article is for a magazine or website – it's for entertainment, rather than for information. So, try to make your writing lively and interesting. Ways you can do this include:

- using direct (rhetorical) questions
- using lots of adjectives and adverbs
- not making the sentences too long and complicated

Remember that in the actual exam your work is assessed on its:

- content (have you done what you're asked to do?)
- language (is your grammar, vocabulary and spelling generally good even if there are some mistakes?)
- organisation (does your writing follow a clear, logical pattern?)
- communication (is your writing in an appropriate style – not too formal or informal?)

Manuela wrote an article after she saw this task:

THE BEST PLACE I'VE EVER VISITED

What's the best place you've ever visited?

When did you go? Who with?
What did you like so much about it?

Write and tell us.
Write about 140–190 words.

We'll publish the best articles on our website! And there are prizes for the winners!

---

1 Read Manuela's article and answer the questions.

1 Does she do everything that the task asks her to do?

_____

2 Find and circle:
a adjectives that she uses
b three 'questions' that she uses

The best place I've ever visited? It has to be Disney World, in Florida. We live in Mexico City and a trip to the USA had always been my dream. On my eleventh birthday, my parents gave me a white envelope instead of the usual present. And can you <u>guess what</u> it was? Of course – our plane tickets to spend six nights in Disney World. <u>I was just so</u> excited!

We flew about five weeks later. <u>I can still remember</u> so many things about that fantastic trip. We stayed in a resort in the Epcot Centre, and every day we went to see something different. I guess my real favourite was the Wild Africa Trek – three hours of walking and seeing wild animals – it was incredible. <u>And then there were</u> the rides, of course – we all got in a raft one afternoon and did some white-water rafting, that was scary but fun, we got drenched!

So we had five days of fun, sun, great food, ice cream, rides – what's not to like? <u>I can hardly wait to</u> go back!

2 Look at the underlined phrases in the article. They are phrases that you could use in this kind of article writing. Can you find at least one other phrase you think you could use?

3 Write an article of your own. You can choose the task that Manuela did, or the one below.

NOMADIC PEOPLE I'D LIKE TO KNOW

There are many nomadic people in the world – e.g. the Inuit and the Tuareg.
If you could meet and spend some time with a nomadic tribe, which one would it be and why?
Write and tell us. Write about 140–190 words.
We'll publish the best articles on our website!
And there are prizes for the winners!

CONSOLIDATION

LISTENING

1 🔊 07 Listen to Amelia talking about her year in Indonesia. Put the things below in the order she mentions them. There are two she doesn't mention.

☐ the food ☐ the language
☐ her school ☐ transport
☐ the weather ☐ the people

2 🔊 07 Listen again and mark the sentences T (true) or F (false).

1 Amelia's dad was only going to spend half a year there. ☐
2 The weather was always hot and dry. ☐
3 Amelia's lost contact with most of her Indonesian friends. ☐
4 She used to buy nasi goreng from a shop. ☐
5 Amelia describes a bejak journey as being a bit dangerous but exciting too. ☐

GRAMMAR

3 Choose the correct option.

1 I don't mind *to help / helping* you with your homework.
2 But, Dad, you promised *to take / taking* me to the cinema tonight!
3 I feel like *to eat / eating* some chocolate. I don't suppose you've got any?
4 Can I suggest *to take / taking* a break and finishing this later?
5 I really regret *to tell / telling* Paul all those things.
6 I bumped into Joshua on the high street and we stopped *to have / having* a chat.
7 I forgot *to post / posting* this letter again.
8 I don't remember *to invite / inviting* Ian to my party. Why's he here?

4 Join the sentences to make one sentence.

1 My sister spends all day on her phone. I find this very annoying.
_____
2 My favourite town is Brighton. It's on the south coast.
_____
3 I watched the film last night. I thought it was really boring.
_____
4 My best friend is Al. He was born on the same day as me.
_____

VOCABULARY

5 Match the sentence halves.

1 I don't know how you put up ☐
2 I'm ashamed of what I said and ☐
3 Housework really wears me ☐
4 I'm a bit stuck and ☐
5 I wasn't in Spain long and I only picked ☐
6 I felt a bit awkward and ☐
7 It was a terrible thing to go ☐
8 I can tell that he's guilty ☐

a out and makes me feel tired.
b through and she doesn't like talking about it.
c didn't know what to say.
d by the look on his face.
e could use some help.
f with all his terrible jokes.
g I want to say sorry.
h up a few words of the language.

6 Complete each word.

1 We had to c_____ on our hands and knees.
2 The r_____ are really unhappy about the plans to open a new nightclub in the area.
3 The c_____ made sure all the passengers were safely off the ship before they left.
4 They w_____ around the city for hours. They had no idea where they were going.
5 She t_____ quietly up the stairs.
6 The a_____ hated his performance and he was booed off stage.
7 The company has more than 1,000 e_____ .
8 He grabbed the rope and s_____ across the river.

UNITS 1 & 2

DIALOGUE

7 Complete the dialogue with the phrases in the list. There are two you won't use.

You know what? | You'll never manage to do it | It's a deal | That's too easy
Same here | Of course I can | I bet you can't | Give me a shout

DAN You can't go for more than an hour without checking your phone.
ANA ¹_____.
DAN No you can't. I mean we've only been in the restaurant 20 minutes and you've already checked it twice.
ANA Well, I'm expecting an important message.
DAN Really? ² _____ I don't think you could survive without your phone. Not even for five minutes. In fact, ³ _____ spend the rest of the meal without your phone.
ANA Don't be silly. ⁴ _____.
DAN Is it? OK, if you don't look at your phone until we finish eating, I'll pay for dinner.
ANA ⁵ _____. I hope you've got a lot of money with you.
DAN I haven't but that's no problem. ⁶ _____.
ANA OK, let's see.

READING

8 Read the article and answer the questions.

You would expect extreme sportspeople to be equipped with survival techniques. A mountaineer needs to be ready for a rapid descent in bad weather and a deep-sea diver needs to know what to do should they ever come face to face with a great white shark, for example. Even more everyday sportspeople need to know a few basic procedures and more than one football player's life has been saved by the actions of a quick-thinking team mate. But if there's one sport you would expect to be pretty safe, then it's golf. Apart from a few sand bunkers and maybe a pond or two, golf courses are hardly the most dangerous of places. Indeed, golf courses are often set in some of the most beautiful countryside there is. What could possibly go wrong there? In fact the only people who might be in danger are the spectators who run the risk of a golf ball landing on their head from time to time.

Swedish golfer Daniela Holmqvist might have a thing or two to say about this. She was in Australia playing in a tournament when she felt a nasty bite on her lower leg. When she looked she saw a small black spider on her ankle. She immediately brushed it away but the pain was getting stronger and stronger. She quickly called for help and was told that she had been bitten by a black widow spider, one of the most poisonous creatures in the world. In fact, one bite can kill an adult in less than an hour. The local people were very concerned and immediately called for medical help. But Daniela knew she could not afford to wait for it. She knew she had to do something there and then as her leg had already started to swell.

From out of her pocket she pulled a tee, the plastic object that a golfer uses to place the ball on at the start of each hole. Using the sharp end of the tee, she made a hole in her leg and squeezed the poison out from inside. It came flowing out in a clear liquid. Despite the pain she kept applying pressure until all the fluid had been removed. Doctors were soon on the scene and helped bandage Daniela up. You might have thought that after a brush with death like this, you would want to go home and rest for a while. Not Daniela: instead of taking any time off to recover, Daniela insisted on finishing the remaining 14 holes to complete her game.

1 What dangers might a mountaineer or a deep-sea diver encounter? _____
2 What dangers might a golfer encounter? _____
3 What danger did Daniela Holmqvist encounter? _____
4 How did she react at first? _____
5 What did she do to survive the danger? _____
6 What did she do once the danger was over? _____

WRITING

9 Think of a dangerous situation and write a paragraph about how you would respond. Write about 180 words.

Include:
- what the situation was
- what you did
- how you felt afterwards

3 THE NEXT GENERATION

GRAMMAR

Quantifiers [SB page 32]

1 ★☆☆ Put the sentences in order (1–4) according to amount, 1 being the most.

1
a She's got loads of cousins. [1]
b She's got a few cousins. [ ]
c She's got several cousins. [ ]
d She's got hardly any cousins. [ ]

2
a A small number of the children at our school go on to university. [ ]
b None of the children at our school go on to university. [ ]
c All of the children at our school go on to university. [ ]
d The vast majority of children at our school go on to university. [ ]

3
a Mum hardly spends any time at home. [ ]
b Mum spends plenty of time at home. [ ]
c Mum doesn't spend much time at home. [ ]
d Mum spends all her time at home. [ ]

2 ★★☆ Complete the text with the words in the list.

loads | number | plenty | most | majority
deal | few | almost | hardly | all of | several

I love the street where we live. There are ⁰ _loads_ of houses and the vast ¹ _____ have families living in them. That means there are always ² _____ of children to play with. There are ³ _____ kids from my class at school and ⁴ _____ us love football so ⁵ _____ days you'll find us playing football in the park at the end of the street. The park is great and I spend ⁶ _____ all of my time there. Of course, there are a small ⁷ _____ of mean kids who hang out there but they don't usually bother us. At the other end of the road there are a ⁸ _____ shops where I spend a good ⁹ _____ of my pocket money on sweets. By Friday evening I've got ¹⁰ _____ any pocket money left!

3 ★★☆ Circle the correct option.

1 My cousin's crazy about cars. He's got *loads of / hardly any / a few* books on them.
2 There's no need to hurry. We've got *several / plenty / the vast majority* of time.
3 *Hardly any / Several / Good deal* of the public trust politicians.
4 Let Phil pay. He's got *most / loads / all* of money.
5 The *vast majority / good deal / most* of children at our school speak two languages.
6 *All / A few / Several* of my cousins went to university so of course, Mum and Dad expect me to go too.

4 ★★★ Choose quantifiers and complete the sentences so they are true for you.

1 I spend _____ my time _____
2 _____ my friends _____
3 _____ the teachers at my school _____
4 _____ the children at my school _____
5 I spend _____ my money _____
6 I find _____ the subjects at school _____

so and *such* (review) [SB page 35]

5 ★★☆ Rewrite the sentences using the word(s) in brackets.

0 This is such a difficult question. (so)
   This question is so difficult.
1 It's such a hot day today. (so)
   _____
2 My uncle's so rich. (such / man)
   _____
3 Dawn's got so many problems. (such / a lot of)
   _____
4 I ate so much. (such)
   _____

6 ★★★ Write continuations for the sentences in Exercise 5.

0 _This question is so difficult that I've no idea what the answer is._

3 THE NEXT GENERATION

too and (not) enough SB page 35

7 ★★☆ Complete the sentence for each picture. Use *too* or *(not) enough*. Sometimes there is more than one possible answer.

0 Sorry, *you're not old enough. / you're too young.*

1 Forget it, _____

   Let's come back later.

2 I can't do it, _____

3 Do you know what your problem is?

do and did for emphasis SB page 35

8 ★☆☆ Match the sentences.

1 Lucy did go to your party.
2 I did enjoy that meal.
3 Paul did seem a little strange.
4 I do wish you'd turn down your music.
5 Jen looks great in that dress.
6 I do really like you.

a Is there anything wrong with him?
b I'm trying to study.
c Green does suit her.
d She was wearing a red dress – remember?
e But not enough to be your girlfriend, sorry.
f But I think I ate too much.

9 ★★☆ Rewrite the sentences adding *do/does* or *did* to make them more emphatic. Make any other necessary changes.

0 So you like my present! I thought you didn't.
   So you do like my present! I thought you didn't.

1 You know Alan. You met him at Steve's party, remember?

2 We spend a lot of our time talking about the same things. It's getting a bit boring.

3 My dad embarrasses me sometimes but I guess all dads do.

4 I don't know what May said but I enjoyed your party.

5 Miss Holloway's great but she talks a lot.

6 I've hardly got any money left. We bought a lot of things today.

7 I miss my mum when she travels abroad for work.

GET IT RIGHT!
so and such

Learners often confuse *so* and *such*.

✓ We had no idea that we were going to become **such** good friends.
✗ We had no idea that we were going to become ~~so~~ good friends.
✓ Luke's parents aren't **so** strict.
✗ Luke's parents aren't ~~such~~ strict.

Find four mistakes in the text. Correct them.

Bringing up children is not an easy job and some parents can be such strict that their children sometimes rebel. There is so a lot of advice out there about raising children that it's not always easy to make the right decisions. Amy Chua's book was such interesting I read it twice and it contained so many useful pieces of advice. Childhood is so a significant time in your life and it's so important to get things right.

VOCABULARY

Word list

Costumes and uniforms

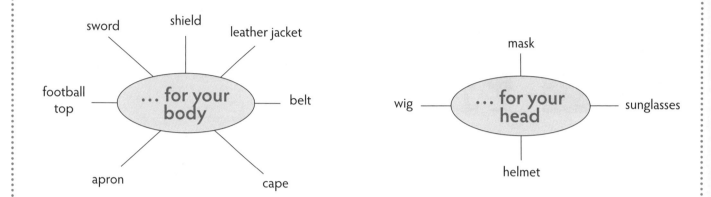

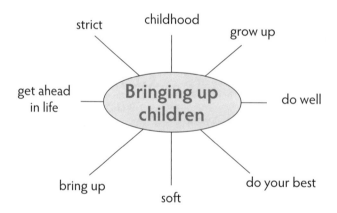

Key words in context

collection	My brother's got a huge **collection** of football shirts.
doorstep	Don't stand there on the **doorstep**. Come in.
fancy-dress	Have you decided what costume to wear to the **fancy-dress** party?
farewell	It's always sad to say **farewell** to colleagues who you've worked with for a number of years.
genius	They're a family of **geniuses**. They're all so intelligent.
ordinary	I'm just an **ordinary** kid like everyone else.
parenting	Good **parenting** is a real skill.
provocative	That was a **provocative** thing to say. Are you looking for an argument?

3 THE NEXT GENERATION

Costumes and uniforms SB page 32

1 ★☆☆ Unscramble the words to make costumes and uniforms. Then match the words with the pictures.

1 giw
2 tleb
3 sesnuslags
4 mehtle
5 words
6 smak
7 delish
8 pace
9 napor

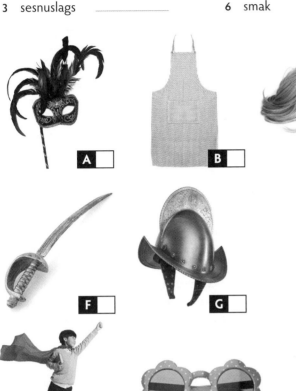

2 ★★☆ Complete the story with words from Exercise 1.

An invitation to a fancy dress party. Cool! What was I going to wear? I thought about going as a chef but Dad's ¹_____ was filthy and I didn't have time to wash it. What about a knight? I could use a stick as a ²_____ and a dustbin lid as a ³_____ but what about a ⁴_____ to wear on my head? No, a knight was too difficult. Then I thought about going as a superhero, a ⁵_____ to cover my face, a big ⁶_____ around my waist and a ⁷_____ over the top. Not bad but then I had a brilliant idea …
I arrived at Mike's house and knocked on the door. I was a rock star and I looked cool! Dark ⁸_____ hiding my eyes, a ⁹_____ of long black hair on my head and my dad's leather jacket.
Mike opened the door dressed in a suit and tie. Tina, his girlfriend was stood beside him in a beautiful dress. He looked at me and laughed. 'When I said dress fancy, I meant dress *smart*,' he laughed. It was too late now. I had to go in …

Bringing up children SB page 35

3 ★☆☆ Match the phrases and the definitions.

1 do well
2 strict
3 do your best
4 bring up
5 soft
6 childhood
7 grow up
8 get ahead in life

a to try your hardest
b to raise (children)
c to describe a parent who doesn't impose a lot of rules on their children
d to be successful
e to get older
f to describe a parent who imposes a lot of rules on their children
g to make good progress at school, in your job, etc.
h the period of your life until the age of 18

4 ★★☆ Circle the correct option.

1 All parents want to help their children *get ahead in life* / *grow up*.
2 It doesn't matter if you win or lose, as long as you *do well* / *do your best*.
3 I had a really happy *childhood* / *bring up*.
4 It was difficult for my dad *growing* / *bringing* up three children on his own.
5 She *did* / *made* really well in her final exam.
6 They can do whatever they want. Their parents are really *soft* / *strict*.
7 My little cousin is *growing* / *bringing* up really quickly.
8 My parents are so *soft* / *strict*. They don't let me do anything.

READING

1 **REMEMBER AND CHECK** Correct the mistakes in these sentences. Then check your answers on page 31 of the Student's Book.

1 Dale stood at the garden gate to wave Rain off.

2 Dale wore fancy dress to wave Rain off to school on his first day at high school.

3 Rain saw that his dad was dressed as an American football player as he was climbing onto the bus.

4 Dale waved Rain off only when the weather was good.

5 Dale got a lot of his costumes from a fancy-dress shop.

6 Rochelle Price took short videos of her husband to put on their website.

7 Rain never really appreciated what his dad did.

8 Dale is looking forward to waving at the bus when school starts after the summer holidays.

2 Read the magazine article. Who is it written by?

A A parent with a difficult teen at home
B A young person with a difficult problem
C Someone who understands typical teenage issues

3 Match the titles with the paragraphs. There are two extra titles.

1 Try and be more understanding
2 Don't get too upset
3 Collect the evidence
4 They don't even know why they do it
5 Choose the behaviour you find most embarrassing
6 Have a family meeting

4 Write a short text describing a problem you had with your parents and how you solved it.

How to survive ... embarrassing parents

Don't get me wrong – I love my parents to bits. I know they love me too and would do anything to help me but sometimes they can be well ... really embarrassing. Dad wanting to pick me up from school, Mum getting over-excited when she watches me playing football for the school team. And I know it's not just me. My friends all moan about theirs from time to time. It seems a few cruel parents deliberately want to see their kids suffer, but others are just trying to be cool and fit in with our friends. Either way, they can make life pretty tricky for us at times. There's not really much we can do about it, or is there? Here are a few tips I've come up with to make life just a little easier for all of us.

A _____

Write a list of all the things you find embarrassing and then put them in order. Is the fact that your dad sings along to the radio when your friends are over for dinner worse than the fact that he always calls your best friend by the wrong name? By deciding which ones are worse means you'll be free to focus your energy where you need it most.

B _____

When you've decided which issues you want to talk about, keep a diary of all the times your mum or dad do the things that embarrass you most. When, where and how you felt – make a note of all these things. They'll help you put your case across.

C _____

When you've got enough evidence, it's time for a little face-to-face chat. Use your notes to help you. The chances are that even if your parents are conscious of doing these things, they probably don't realise how embarrassing they are. Keep calm. Let them know how you feel and why. Let them have their say – they'll probably want to defend themselves. Of course, you'll also have to be prepared to listen to some of the things that they're not so keen on about your behaviour. It's part of the deal. Maybe you can both agree to think more carefully about some of your actions.

D _____

Hopefully your parents will listen and be willing to change their ways, especially if you say you're happy to change too. Of course, sometimes they might not. When this happens then the best advice I can offer is to ignore it and get on with your life. If you do this, things will be a lot easier. Remember that they once had their own embarrassing parents, and the chances are many of us will be embarrassing parents ourselves one day. Maybe we shouldn't be too hard on them.

3 THE NEXT GENERATION

DEVELOPING WRITING

An essay about the role of grandparents

1 Read the essay and answer the questions.

1 Why does the writer think grandparents are more active in their grandchildren's lives these days?
2 Why can this be a good thing?
3 What should parents be careful about?

Grandparents can play an important part in children's lives. Do you agree?

Because of the high costs of professional child care, more and more parents in the UK are relying on their own mothers and fathers to look after their children so that they can go back to work. This means that these grandparents are getting to spend far more time with their grandchildren than their own parents did, but is this always a good thing?

Of course, grandparents can be a wonderful influence in a child's life. No one, except for their own parents, can love them more and the children will generally be well cared for. The time and attention that the child receives will help them grow up securely, knowing that they are special. This relationship often continues in later years and many teenagers have a close bond with their grandparents, knowing that they can turn to them with problems they won't always want to share with their parents.

But parents shouldn't abuse this situation. Parents should always be the most important influence in any child's life. They need to be there and make the important decisions rather than rely upon their own mothers and fathers to do so for them. To sum up, children who grow up having a close relationship with their grandparents are very lucky indeed. However, their parents must be careful not to forget their responsibility for their child's upbringing and happiness.

2 Complete these sentences from the essay with the missing words. Then check in the text. What effect do these words have on the sentences?

1 This means that these grandparents are getting to spend _____ more time with their grandchildren than their own parents did.
2 _____ _____, grandparents can be a wonderful influence in a child's life.
3 Parents should _____ be the most important influence in any child's life.
4 To sum up, children who grow up having a close relationship with their grandparents are very lucky _____.

3 Use the missing words from Exercise 2 to make these sentences more emphatic. Sometimes there is more than one possibility.

1 You must think of the child's safety.
2 It's more difficult to spend all day looking after young children.
3 Grandparents love their grandchildren very much.
4 Grandparents want to help their own children.

4 Make notes to answer the questions.

1 What is the role of grandparents in your society?
2 What is good about the situation?
3 Is there anything to be careful about?
4 What are your thoughts?

5 Use your notes to write an answer to the essay question in about 200 words.

CHECKLIST

- Include an attention-grabbing introduction
- Organise your ideas in a logical sequence
- Include examples of emphatic language
- Read through your essay to check for mistakes

LISTENING

1 🔊08 Listen and write the name of the embarrassed daughter (Jen, Sue or Dawn) under the picture of the dad.

A ☐

B ☐

C ☐

2 🔊08 Listen again and mark the sentences T (true) or F (false).

1 Jen never needs a lift from her dad. ☐
2 Jen's mum is sympathetic to her daughter's complaint. ☐
3 Sue thinks her dad's hairstyle is old-fashioned. ☐
4 Sue's mum is sympathetic to her daughter's complaint. ☐
5 Dawn's taste in music has changed. ☐
6 Dawn's mum is sympathetic to her daughter's complaint. ☐

3 🔊08 Make the sentences more emphatic by rewriting them with *do*, *so* or *such* in the correct form. Listen again and check.

1 Dad knows how to embarrass me.
   _____
2 We're your parents, Jen, we care about you.
   _____
3 It's an inappropriate hairstyle for a man of his age.
   _____
4 Dad's embarrassing.
   _____
5 I liked it when I was about eight.
   _____

DIALOGUE

1 Put the dialogue in order.

☐ DAD Well it's our house and we like to keep it just a little bit tidy.
☐ DAD It's your bedroom. It's such a mess. Again.
☐ DAD Because maybe when I go to check your room in half an hour it will be perfect.
☐ DAD Very funny, Paul. Now I did say that if your room was a mess, I wouldn't give you your pocket money this month.
[1] DAD You do know how to annoy your mum, Paul.
☐ DAD I can but maybe I won't need to.
☐ PAUL It will be, Dad. Thanks for the second chance.
☐ PAUL Well, it's my bedroom so I don't see what the problem is.
☐ PAUL Why not?
☐ PAUL A bit tidy? This house is so tidy we could invite the Queen round for dinner.
☐ PAUL What have I done now?
☐ PAUL No way, Dad, you can't do that. I need the money.

2 Use the words in brackets to change the sentences and make them more emphatic.

MUM Why didn't you clean your room?
JAY But I cleaned it, Mum. (did)
1 _____

MUM Really? Last time I looked it was a mess. (such)
2 _____

JAY When was that?
MUM Five minutes ago!
JAY Well go and have a look now. It's tidy. You won't believe it. (so)
3 _____

MUM And if I look under the bed?
JAY Mum, you know how to be annoying, don't you? Just give me five more minutes then.

3 Write a short dialogue (6–10 lines) between a parent and child. Use at least two examples of emphatic language.

Pronunciation
Adding emphasis
Go to page 118. 🔊

CAMBRIDGE ENGLISH: First

Listening part 3

1 🔊 10 You will hear five short extracts in which people are talking about family holidays. For questions 1–5, choose from the list (A–H) what each speaker says about them. Use the letters only once. There are three extra letters which you do not need to use.

A They're never as good as I hope they will be.
B They're usually very stressful.
C Everyone does what they want to do.
D My parents worry too much about showing us a good time.
E It's a good time to reconnect with everyone.
F Mum and Dad can never really relax on them.
G We never go to places that I want to go to.
H I think I've outgrown them.

Speaker 1 ☐
Speaker 2 ☐
Speaker 3 ☐
Speaker 4 ☐
Speaker 5 ☐

Exam guide: multiple matching

In this part of the exam you need to match speakers to a sentence describing part of what they are talking about.

- You hear five people talking about the same subject – they are not connected to each other. You hear each extract twice.
- On the exam paper there are eight comments. Your job is to match one to each of the speakers. There are three comments you won't use.
- Before you listen, read through the comments to prepare yourself for the sorts of things you will hear.
- You will need to listen out for attitudes, opinions, purpose, feelings, main points and details.
- Listen to each speaker carefully. You will sometimes hear things that are intended to distract you from the correct answer, so avoid making quick decisions.
- Use your second listening to confirm answers you have already chosen and answer those questions you weren't able to the first time round.

2 🔊 11 You will hear five short extracts in which people are answering the question, 'What is the most important role of a parent?' For questions 1–5, choose from the list (A–H) what each speaker says about it. Use the letters only once. There are three extra letters which you do not need to use.

A Parents need to ensure that they supply their children with the fundamental requirements.
B Parents have to expect they will have difficult times with their teenage children.
C Parents need to teach their children values.
D Survival skills are the most important thing a parent can pass on to their child.
E Parents can never be really good friends with their children.
F The most important part of being a parent comes naturally.
G It's very difficult to choose which role is most essential.
H Parents need to take more responsibility.

Speaker 1 ☐
Speaker 2 ☐
Speaker 3 ☐
Speaker 4 ☐
Speaker 5 ☐

35

4 THINKING OUTSIDE THE BOX

GRAMMAR
be / get used to (doing) vs. used to (do) SB page 40

1 ★☆☆ Complete with the correct form of the verb given (infinitive or -ing form).

1 That fast food place used to _____ my favourite French restaurant. (be)
2 When I first lived in a flat I couldn't get used to _____ our neighbour's music. (hear)
3 My mother has finally got used to _____ the Internet on her phone. (have)
4 Pedro comes from Brazil, so he isn't used to _____ British food. (eat)
5 Sheila used to _____ jeans all the time when she was a student. (wear)
6 We live near the palace and we're very used to _____ members of the royal family going past. (see)
7 I wonder if I'll ever get used to _____ in such a beautiful place. (live)
8 When we arrived in London, we weren't used to _____ in so much traffic. (drive)

2 ★★☆ Circle the correct option.

When I was young I ¹*used to / got used to* play outside with my friends. My mum ²*used to / was used to* me going out to ride my bike with them. Sometimes I was out for hours, but she ³*used to / got used to* that, too. We often rode on mud tracks that ⁴*used to / were used to* be used by motorcyclists, and they were often wet and slippery so I ⁵*used to / got used to* falling off my bike a lot. And so my mum ⁶*used to / was used to* seeing me covered with mud and bruises.
Now I ⁷*used to / am used to* driving safely in my car and staying clean! I don't think I could ⁸*be used to / get used to* riding a bike again now.

3 ★★☆ Complete the sentences with the correct form of *be* or *get*.

1 Julia is Mexican so she _____ used to hot weather.
2 My uncle's working in Berlin, so he had to _____ used to different food.
3 It never takes me long to _____ used to being in another country.
4 My father lived in Italy for years, but he never _____ used to driving on the right.
5 My grandmother _____ used to living in her small flat now, and she's very happy.
6 Bernard grew up in Norway. As a child he _____ used to skiing to school.
7 I like warm weather. I could never _____ used to very cold winters.
8 People in some parts of Japan _____ used to experiencing earthquakes – they happen quite often.
9 On holiday, I went to the beach every day. That's something I could easily _____ used to!

4 ★★★ Complete the statements. Make them true for you.

1 When I was younger I used to
_____
2 When I started school it wasn't easy to get used to
_____
3 Now I am used to
_____
4 My best friend was used to
_____
before I met him/her.
5 My parents have never got used to
_____

36

4 THINKING OUTSIDE THE BOX

Adverbs and adverbial phrases
SB page 43

5 ★☆☆ Complete the sentences with the adverb formed from the adjective in brackets.

0 The horse jumped over all the barriers *easily*. (easy)
1 The car was going too _____ for the police to catch up with. (fast)
2 The singer sang the song _____. (beautiful)
3 Matty didn't do the test _____ enough to get top marks. (good)
4 My eyes _____ became accustomed to the dim light. (slow)
5 Sam worked really _____ to finish the job on time. (hard)

6 ★☆☆ Complete the sentences with a word from the list.

enjoyable | different | surprise | friendly
interest | excitement | fear | strange

1 We really like Ms Philips, she teaches PE in an _____ way.
2 We all jumped with _____ when the door slammed.
3 She came second, but she congratulated the winner in a _____ way.
4 The fans screamed with _____ when the pop group walked onto the stage.
5 Nobody understood the teacher's explanation of calculus, until he explained it in a _____ way.
6 Fran started to shake with _____ when she looked over the edge of the cliff.
7 The dog was walking in a _____ way because he had hurt his paw.
8 Harry told us a long, boring story which we listened to without much _____.

7 ★★★ Complete the sentences with a phrase. Make them true for you.

1 I watch _____ on TV _____
2 I do my homework _____
3 I read books _____
4 I always try to _____ in a friendly way.
5 I like to _____ in a different way.
6 I admire people who _____ without fear.
7 I know someone who walks _____
8 I go to the maths class _____

8 ★★★ Write complete sentences from the prompts. Use adverbial phrases and make any other necessary changes.

0 Mary / ask / her hairdresser / style / her hair / different
   Mary asked her hairdresser to style her hair in a different way.

1 Jack / approach / lion / fear

2 Candy / carry / three suitcases / difficulty

3 The boys / eat / hamburgers / enthusiasm

4 Jerry / ride / horse / awkward

5 Helen / watch / football match / interest

GET IT RIGHT!
Adverbs

Learners often make word order errors with adverbs.
✓ You can **easily find** a hotel.
✗ You can ~~find easily~~ a hotel.

Put the words in order to make sentences.

1 finish / by / I'll / project / next / definitely / the / Monday

2 immediately / you / It's / thing / good / that / came / a

3 your / I / view / understand / point / totally / of

4 and / Dan / on / hard / his / got / worked / top / homework / marks

5 Jo and Kate / would / hear / quietly / so / speaking / no one / were / them

6 job / creatively / to / in / Do / always / think / have / your / you / ?

7 locally / so / I / home / walk / live / I / can

8 eaten / probably / pizza / the / This / I've / is / best / ever

37

VOCABULARY

Word list

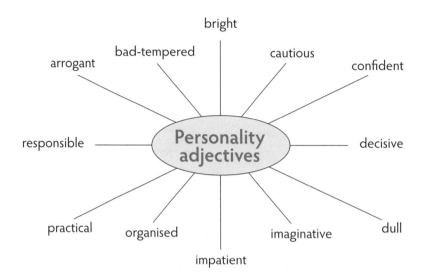

Common adverbial phrases
by accident
in a hurry
in a panic
in a row
in private
in public
in secret
on purpose

good
for good
it's a good thing
it's all good
it's no good
not very good at
so far, so good

Key words in context

anxious	I've never acted on stage before, so right now I'm a bit **anxious**.
brainstorm	We need some new, fresh ideas – let's **brainstorm** for ten minutes or so.
capable	Sometimes we find that we are **capable** of more things than we think we are.
charge	My phone battery's dead – I need to **charge** it.
conflict	They argue with each other all the time – there's a lot of **conflict** between them.
enthusiasm	She didn't really want to go, so she didn't watch the play with any **enthusiasm**.
flash	A police car went past with a blue **flashing** light on its roof.
on the basis (that)	We chose him for the basketball team **on the basis that** he was the tallest guy we knew.
scholarship	She isn't paying for her course because she won a **scholarship**.

4 THINKING OUTSIDE THE BOX

Personality adjectives SB page 40

1 ★★☆ Complete the puzzle. Read what each person says and write the adjective to describe the person. Find the mystery word.

1. I learn quickly and easily.
2. I get lots of new ideas.
3. If I say I'll do something, then I do it.
4. I'm the best, by far!
5. I always think carefully before I do anything.
6. I'm sure of my abilities.
7. I don't sit around thinking for a long time.
8. I know where everything is.
9. I'm better at doing things than thinking about things.

Mystery word: 'I want it – and I want it now!'

2 ★★☆ Complete with an appropriate adjective.

1. A She gets angry at everything I say.
   B Oh, I know, she's quite _____.
2. A He drives quite slowly.
   B Yes, he's a _____ driver, usually.
3. A She designs such different, interesting things!
   B Yes, she's very _____.
4. A Let's go to Australia for our holiday.
   B Oh, be _____. We haven't got enough money for that.
5. A Do you think she'll do what she promised?
   B Oh yes – she's very _____.
6. A She thinks she's the best. I guess she's confident.
   B No, it's more than that – she's really _____.
7. A Hurry up!
   B OK. Don't be so _____!
8. A He isn't very interesting, is he?
   B No, he's a bit _____, really.

Common adverbial phrases SB page 43

3 ★☆☆ Complete the sentences with the phrases in the list.

by accident | in a hurry | in a panic | in a row
in public | in secret | on purpose | in private

1. Sorry, I can't stop and talk now – I'm _____.
2. I made a mistake – I clicked the wrong button and deleted the file _____.
3. I'm a nervous person – I don't think I could ever make a speech _____.
4. Has any country ever won the World Cup three times _____?
5. I only ever sing _____ – in the shower, for example.
6. No one knew that the meetings were happening – they were held _____.
7. I was so worried about being late that I started to do everything _____.
8. I'm sorry I broke it, but I promise you, I didn't do it _____!

WordWise SB page 45
good

4 ★★☆ Use phrases with *good* to complete the sentences.

0. No school today, the sun's shining, I'm with my friends – *it's all good*.
1. She's not going to Australia just for a holiday – she's going there _____.
2. Oh, no! This food is awful! Well, I guess I'm _____ at cooking.
3. A It's really cold today.
   B Yes. _____ we're wearing our coats.
4. A How are you getting on?
   B _____. I think I'll finish in ten minutes.
5. I've apologised three times to her, but _____ – she's still angry with me.

5 ★★★ Complete the sentences so that they are true for you.

1. I'm not very good at _____.
2. It's a good thing that I _____.
3. I'm going to _____ for good.
4. I would really like to _____ but it's no good.

READING

1 **REMEMBER AND CHECK** Mark the sentences T (true) or F (false). Then check your answers in the article on page 39 of the Student's Book.

1. Richard is a member of the Zulu tribe.
2. The tribe had problems because lions were killing people.
3. Richard's first idea was to use fire to keep the lions away.
4. The lions did not like a moving light.
5. To make his light, Richard used a battery from an old motorbike.
6. Richard designed a light that flashed all night.
7. Lions no longer kill Richard's father's animals.
8. Because of his idea, Richard now teaches at a college in the USA.

2 Read the article. Find three things that Einstein believed in as being important for thinking.

Einstein's thinking

'The true sign of intelligence is not knowledge, but imagination.' *Albert Einstein*

For a lot of people, one of the best examples of creative genius was Albert Einstein, the physicist who came up with the Theory of Relativity, and by doing so, changed physics forever. However, what a lot of people don't know is that Einstein had specific techniques that he used to develop his ability to think creatively and freely.

Possibility thinking

The main approach that Einstein took was something he called 'possibility thinking' – in other words, letting yourself imagine things that are often way outside reality, and pushing the limits of what you know. It means getting away from our familiar thoughts and ideas and trying to imagine many other possible things, no matter how incredible they might seem.

Einstein had a special technique to do this, which he called 'the thought experiment'. This example of possibility thinking is simply an experiment that you do inside your own head. Perhaps the most famous thought experiment is the one that Einstein says he used to get himself on the path towards the Theory of Relativity. Einstein was interested in light and the speed of light and its relationship to time, so what he did was to imagine himself riding on a beam of sunlight. Now, that's an impossible thing to do, of course, but Einstein said that using his imagination like this allowed him to understand some of the relationships between light and time, and how they work.

Essentially, how we experience time depends on where we are and what we are doing. Einstein explained it as follows: 'When you're talking to a pretty girl, an hour seems like a minute. If you sit on a hot fire, a minute seems like an hour. That's relativity.'

Time for creative thinking

But importantly, for possibility thinking to be effective, we have to give ourselves opportunities to practise it. Lots of people say that their 'thinking time' is when they're taking a bath, or when they're on the bus to work or school. But Einstein believed that it is important to devote a period of time every day to 'creative thinking': whatever problem or idea it is that interests you, set aside some time every day to thinking about it – concentrated thinking. And he was a great believer in images, too – he said that he often thought 'in a stream of pictures', and that this was a powerful way to think.

Einstein also believed in thinking about a problem for a long time and not giving up: as he once said, 'I think and think for months and years. Ninety-nine times, the conclusion is false. The hundredth time I am right.'

3 Read the article again. Match the sentence halves.

1. Einstein is known as the genius who
2. Not everybody knows that Einstein
3. Possibility thinking means
4. Einstein came up with an image
5. The image helped him
6. Possibility thinking only really works
7. Einstein felt that thinking in pictures
8. Einstein thought it was important

a. develop his Theory of Relativity.
b. to keep thinking until you get the answer.
c. first thought of the Theory of Relativity.
d. had things that he did to help him think freely.
e. was something very powerful.
f. of himself travelling on a beam of light.
g. moving away from the ways that we usually think.
h. if we practise it regularly.

4 When and where are you able to think the most freely? Write a short paragraph.

Pronunciation

Pronouncing words with *gh*
Go to page 119.

4 THINKING OUTSIDE THE BOX

DEVELOPING WRITING

Writing an email of advice

1 Read Marnie's email. What does she want her sister Becca to do?

Hi Becca,

[A] How are things with you? How's it going at university? I hope you're enjoying everything and not working too hard!

[B] Well, <u>you know that</u> I'm going to be doing my end-of-year exams soon, right? Just like you did all those years ago. <u>Well</u>, I'm writing to ask you for some advice. <u>The thing is</u>, I just can't get going with revision, because I'm really busy with lots of things at school and at home. <u>Now</u>, I know that revision's really, really important, but I'm finding that days are going past and I'm not fitting it in. It's really frustrating. I try to organise my time, but it's hopeless! I'm just useless at it. I also don't really have any techniques for it and I think I'll never come up with anything.

[C] Have you got any tips you can give me?

[D] Now, I know you're busy too but I'm hoping you can find a few minutes to help your sweet younger sister out! The thing is, I don't know who else to ask.

See you soon I hope!

Love

Marnie

---

2 Match the underlined phrases in the email to the definitions.

1 We use this phrase to introduce our main concern or problem. _____
2 We use this phrase to start talking about something the reader/listener already knows. _____
3 We use this word to give emphasis to what we are about to say. _____
4 We use this word to signal we're going to talk about something important. _____

3 Use the underlined phrases in the email to complete the sentences.

1 Sandra – _____ there's a test tomorrow, right?
2 I'd like to give you some advice, but _____, I'm no good at revision myself!
3 So why am I writing? _____, because you asked for my advice, of course!
4 _____, you might not like all these ideas, but I'm going to send them anyway.

4 Match the information to the paragraphs A–D.

1 The main body of the email – the problem. ☐
2 Explaining that you don't want to cause the person a lot of problems, and why you're writing. ☐
3 Saying what you want the reader to do. ☐
4 Some personal exchange about the other person's life. ☐

5 Here are some ideas of how to help Marnie. Add two more ideas of your own. Cross through any that you don't like.

- Revise early in the day; it's better than at night.
- Make a timetable for every day. Tell other people when you're going to do revision.
- Ask someone to test you as soon as you've done some revision.
- Make sure to be away from computers, laptops, tablets, etc. when you revise.
- Put revision notes around the house so you keep seeing them.
- Keep as healthy as you can.
- _____
- _____

6 Imagine you are Becca. Write your reply to Marnie. Use your ideas in Exercise 5. Write 150–200 words.

CHECKLIST ✓

☐ Use a structure for an email
☐ Include some personal exchanges in your introduction
☐ Use some expressions from Exercise 3
☐ Give the most useful advice and say why
☐ Close the email in a friendly way, e.g. *Good luck! / I'm sure you'll do great / I hope this is helpful*

LISTENING

1 🔊 14 Listen and write the number of the conversation next to the correct picture.

A

B

C

2 🔊 14 Listen again and complete the summaries of the conversations. Use between 1 and 3 words.

Conversation 1

The man is trying to ¹_____ his anorak but he can't. The woman offers to help, but he decides to try again. Then he begins to ²_____ so the woman tells him to calm down. Then she tries but she can't ³_____ either. So he decides to ⁴_____ his head but it gets ⁵_____ again. The woman laughs.

Conversation 2

A boy who is painting asks his friend for her opinion. She says it isn't ⁶_____ his last one. Then she admits that ⁷_____ that good. The boy says that he's going to ⁸_____ painting but the girl tries to persuade him not to. But he says that he will ⁹_____ photography and never wants to ¹⁰_____ paints and brushes again.

Conversation 3

A woman needs to think of ¹¹_____ for her company. She has to have them for a meeting ¹²_____ morning, but she's stuck. And she's worried because ¹³_____ o'clock and she might have to ¹⁴_____ late. Her friend starts to tell her about ¹⁵_____ thinking, but she isn't interested so he ¹⁶_____ to it.

DIALOGUE

1 Put the dialogues in the correct order.

1

	JEAN	I'm doing a crossword puzzle and I've only got three answers left to find.
1	JEAN	This is so frustrating!
	JEAN	No chance! I can't give up like that. That would be cheating.
	JEAN	Oh, that's OK. I always prefer to do them on my own, anyway. But I'm really stuck right now.
	MARCUS	A crossword? I'm no good at those. I can't help you, I'm afraid.
	MARCUS	OK then. Well, good luck, tell me when you've finished it!
	MARCUS	What is it? What are you trying to do?
	MARCUS	Well, if you're stuck, why don't you just look at the answers? No one will know!

2

	ELLA	Yes, I am. Well, I'm trying to. But to be honest, I can't do it.
	ELLA	Oh, don't be like that. You're good at these things, usually.
1	ELLA	Hello? James, is that you?
	ELLA	Well, now I give up. I was hoping you might help me! That's why I called.
	JAMES	I know I am. That's why I'm so frustrated. I've tried everything, but it's hopeless.
	JAMES	Hi, Ella. How are you? Are you doing the homework?
	JAMES	I'm stuck, too. I'll never get it right, I'm sure.
	JAMES	Sorry, but there you go. I'll see you tomorrow, Ella. Bye.

PHRASES FOR FLUENCY SB page 45

1 Circle the correct options.

1 **A** This is terrible. I'm starting to panic!
  B OK, *just calm down / you can't be serious*, it'll be OK.

2 **A** Your hair looks awful!
  B You know, *you're really out of order / that's just it* when you say things like that.

3 **A** It's so difficult to find a good babysitter these days.
  B *That's just it / Give it a rest*, no one's available at short notice!

4 **A** Come on, write it down.
  B Sorry, but how do you spell it *off / again*?

5 **A** Honestly – my dad was an international footballer!
  B Oh, *calm down / give it a rest*!

6 **A** I'm going for a swim in the sea.
  B But it's freezing! *You're out of order / You can't be serious*!

CAMBRIDGE ENGLISH: First

Writing part 2

1 Read the exam task. Then read Roberta's letter. Circle the most appropriate options (not too informal).

> Next month you're going to stay with an English-speaking family on an exchange programme. The family's mother has written to you and asked you to say if there's anything she needs to know about you before you go and stay. Write your response.

¹Hi / Dear Mrs Stevens,

²Thank you so much / Thanks a lot for your really kind letter. It was nice to hear from you and I'm really looking forward to meeting you next month.

³Just thought I'd drop you a line / I'm writing now because you asked me if there was anything you should know before I come. Well, I'm quite an easy-going person, so I don't think I'm going to be much trouble! But there are ⁴a couple of / two things that I'd like you to know.

First of all, I sometimes have trouble sleeping and that's especially true if the bedroom isn't very dark. When we go away, I sometimes take an eye-mask with me, but I don't find it comfortable. So, if my room could be nice and dark, that would be ⁵great / cool.

The other thing is food – ⁶I'm not very keen on / I really can't stand spicy food. So if you are all curry fans, I'm afraid I might have to pass! But otherwise, I'll eat ⁷any old stuff / almost anything. (Oh, except mushrooms – sorry!)

I hope this is helpful – please let me know if you need anything else before I arrive.

⁸Best wishes / See you soon

Roberta

2 Read these phrases that people use in letters/emails. Circle the one in each pair that is more formal.

1. A Great to hear from you!
   B Thank you for your letter.
2. A I hope you're well.
   B How are things with you?
3. A Is there anything else I can tell you?
   B What else do you want to know?
4. A I think that's everything.
   B OK, I'm going to wrap up now.
5. A See you!
   B I hope to see you soon.

3 Use the letter to find the answers to the questions Roberta asked herself before writing.

1. How can I reassure Mrs Stevens that there aren't any problems?

2. Should I tell her about my sleeping problem?

3. What, if anything, do I want to say about food? Do I mention spicy food and mushrooms?

4. How can I end the letter in a nice way?

Exam guide: writing a neutral/less informal letter

In part 2 you have to answer one of three questions. You have to write an article, an email/letter, an essay, a review or a story in 140–190 words.

- Think about who you are writing to and the kind of language you should use.
- Plan what you want to say and how you will organise the content of your letter.
- Make sure you start and end the letter with appropriate expressions.
- Make sure you include anything the task tells you to include.

4 Read the letter-writing task below. Plan and write your letter in 140–190 words.

> You spent some time studying English in a school in Britain or the USA. You have received this letter from the school director. Write your answer in 140–190 words in an appropriate style.

> Dear ...
>
> I am writing to tell you that your exam results have arrived – you got an A. Congratulations, it's a great result!
> I was wondering if you would like to return to us here at the school, and study for the examination at the next level up. We feel sure you would do very well in it.
> Please write and let me know.
> Best wishes
> Julia Stevenson

Write your letter.

CONSOLIDATION

LISTENING

1 🔊 15 **Listen to Paul talking about his childhood and circle the correct answers.**

1 Who used to argue the most in his family home?
   A Paul with his parents
   B Paul with his sister and brother
   C Paul's mum with his dad
2 What did Paul think was great about how his parents raised him?
   A They weren't very strict with him.
   B They always had clear expectations.
   C They were always happy to play board games.
3 How did they treat his friends?
   A They weren't very friendly.
   B They were too interfering with them.
   C They wanted to know about them as people.

2 🔊 15 **Listen again and mark the sentences T (true) or F (false).**

1 Paul doesn't remember his parents ever fighting. ☐
2 Paul thinks his parents were too strict at times. ☐
3 Paul couldn't join in with some of the conversations in the school playground. ☐
4 Paul's parents encouraged him to be active. ☐
5 Paul's dad would sometimes embarrass him. ☐

GRAMMAR

3 Put the words in order to make sentences.

1 own / The / of / tablet / friends / vast / my / majority / have / their
   _____
2 board game / We / enough / tonight / players / got / for / haven't / the
   _____
3 that / so / fix / practical / he / anything / He / can / is
   _____
4 to / I / do / do / listening / nothing / to / when / I've / music / enjoy / got
   _____
5 never / I'll / early / to / waking / used / up / get / so
   _____
6 teaches / White / way / chemistry / an / Mr / enjoyable / in
   _____

VOCABULARY

4 Choose the correct options.

1 We didn't recognise him because he was wearing a *mask* / *belt*.
2 Steve is so *arrogant* / *cautious*. He thinks he's better than all of us.
3 Knights carried a *shield* / *sword* to protect themselves from arrows.
4 Cyclists should wear *an apron* / *a helmet* to protect their head.
5 My dad's not very *confident* / *decisive*. He can never make up his mind.
6 He hasn't got any hair so he wears a *cape* / *wig*.
7 Don't be so *impatient* / *dull*. I'll be ready to go in five minutes.
8 Her teachers says she's very *responsible* / *bright* and should go on to university.

5 Match the sentences.

1 My dad's not very strict. ☐
2 Your homework's full of silly mistakes. ☐
3 I had a really happy childhood. ☐
4 He didn't do that by accident. ☐
5 Bring your children up as well as you can. ☐
6 She's a very secretive woman. ☐
7 Our football team's doing really well. ☐
8 Always try and do your best at school. ☐

a It will help you get ahead in life.
b It will help them do well in life.
c He did it on purpose.
d She lives her life in private.
e In fact he's quite soft actually.
f They've won five games in a row now.
g I grew up with a lot of love and care.
h You did it in a hurry, didn't you?

UNITS 3 & 4

DIALOGUE

6 Put the dialogue in the correct order.

	DAD	OK, calm down. You always give up too easily.
	DAD	What do you mean, give up? What do you have to do?
	DAD	Music and art. That sounds perfect for you.
1	DAD	What's the matter, Oscar?
	DAD	That's a bit out of order. I'm only trying to help.
	DAD	No you're not. You just need a good idea.

	OSCAR	I have to design a CD cover for my favourite band.
	OSCAR	I know. I'm sorry, Dad. Maybe I just need a bit of a break.
	OSCAR	That's the problem, Dad. I just can't come up with anything. It's hopeless!
	OSCAR	Leave it out, Dad. Just leave me alone.
6	OSCAR	That's what I thought. But I'm useless.
	OSCAR	It's this school art project. I give up.

READING

7 Read the article and answer the questions.

A work-life balance

For a lot of parents, getting the balance between family life and work is a difficult thing to do. Of course, all parents want to spend time with their children and watch them grow up but at the same time there is the need to make money to provide for the family. Being at work usually means being away from the family and this is often a source of guilt for working mums and dads. One such parent was Mohamed El-Erian.

One night when he asked his ten-year-old daughter to go and brush her teeth before bed, he could have hardly known that it would eventually lead to him resigning as the boss of one of the biggest financial companies in the world.

It seemed that his daughter was ignoring his request and although he asked her several times she just stayed doing what she was doing. Clearly this annoyed her father who wanted to know why she was behaving so badly. When he pointed out that there was a time when she would have obeyed him immediately with no question, she asked him to wait a minute while she fetched something from her bedroom.

What she brought back would make him re-evaluate his life forever, because it was a list of 22 of the most important occasions in her life that he had been absent from. Among them were her first day at school, parents' evening at her school, her first match in the school football team and a holiday parade.

Mohamed immediately had to reassess his life. His high-profile job involved an incredible amount of time out of the house as he arrived in his office each day at 4.15 am and returned home only at 7 pm in time to kiss his daughter good night.

As he read through the list he also realised that he had had an excuse for missing each of the events; an important phone call, travel, urgent meetings, sudden problems that needed his direct involvement. He knew that he had lost control of the balance between his work and his family and that he was neglecting to give his daughter the time and attention that he knew she needed.

As a result he resigned from his job in order to spend more quality time with his family. Although he still works within the industry, he makes sure that he has the flexibility to always be around when he is needed.

Mohamed was just lucky that he got his warning before it was too late and he'd missed his daughter's childhood completely.

1 What was it about his daughter's behaviour that concerned Mohamed El-Erian?

2 How did his daughter respond to his complaint?

3 What excuses did he give for missing the key moments in her life?

4 What did his daughter's list help him realise?

5 How has his life changed?

WRITING

8 Write a paragraph of about 120 words about an occasion in a child's life that no parent should ever miss. Say:

- what the occasion is
- why it's so important
- why the parents should be there

PRONUNCIATION

UNIT 1
Diphthongs: alternative spellings

1 Say the words and write them in the table.

al<u>low</u> | alth<u>ough</u> | ate | boil | climb | de<u>ci</u>de
en<u>joy</u> | height | high | hole | how | join
know | loud | noise | shout | straight
tip<u>toe</u> | wait | weight

/eɪ/ rain	/aɪ/ pie	/əʊ/ coat	/aʊ/ out	/ɔɪ/ boy
			all<u>ow</u>	

2 ◁))03 Listen, check and repeat.

UNIT 2
Phrasal verb stress

1 Tick the sentence in each pair which includes a phrasal verb. Then mark the word you think will be most stressed in each of the underlined phrases for all of the sentences.

0 What are you going to <u>wear to</u> the party?

   After PE today we were all <u>worn out</u>! ✓

1 They <u>had to pick a</u> colour for their team. ☐
   She <u>picked up</u> French really easily. ☐

2 The cake I made yesterday <u>turned out</u> to be delicious! ☐
   Can you <u>turn and</u> face the board, please? ☐

3 I <u>want to hang</u> a picture on that wall. ☐
   I always <u>hang out with</u> my friends on Saturdays. ☐

4 Sarah's ill; she's <u>going through</u> a difficult time. ☐
   We're <u>going to the</u> city to see a play; would you like to come? ☐

5 I think it's better if we <u>all bring our own</u> food to the party. ☐
   Spring <u>brings about</u> many changes in the countryside. ☐

6 I don't know <u>where to put</u> the papers they've left behind. ☐
   My neighbours make a lot of noise but I just have to <u>put up with</u> it. ☐

Remember: We stress the particle in a phrasal verb more than the verb because it's very important – it changes the meaning of the verb.

2 ◁))05 Listen, check and repeat.

UNIT 3
Adding emphasis

1 ◁))09 Rewrite the sentences adding *so*, *such*, *do*, *does* or *did*. Listen and check your answers.

0 Jack McDonald's a good football player!
   Jack McDonald's such a good football player!

1 John gets on well with his parents.
   _____

2 We had a fantastic holiday!
   _____

3 It may not seem like it, but he likes you.
   _____

4 I didn't pass the test – but I studied hard.
   _____

5 What a wonderful day – I love it when the sun's shining!
   _____

2 Try saying the sentences with and without *so*, *such*, *do*, *does* and *did*. What difference do you notice?

3 ◁))09 Listen again and repeat the sentences with *so*, *such*, *do*, *does* and *did*.

PRONUNCIATION

UNIT 4
Pronouncing words with *gh*

1 Write the words in the table.

although | brought | caught | cough | daughter
enough | fight | ghost | height | high | laugh
light | straight | thought | tough | through | weigh

gh silent	*gh* pronounced /f/	*gh* pronounced /g/
although		

2 🔊 12 Listen, check and repeat.

3 Match the words in the list that rhyme with words a–l below.

sport | buy | half | late | off | play | stuff
taught | toast | you | water | white

a thought   *sport*
b laugh   _____
c enough   _____
d through   _____
e ghost   _____
f high   _____
g straight   _____
h height   _____
i weigh   _____
j brought   _____
k daughter   _____
l cough   _____

4 🔊 13 Listen, check and repeat.

GRAMMAR REFERENCE

UNIT 1

Verb patterns: *to* + infinitive or gerund

1 When a verb is followed by another verb, the second verb is either in the gerund form (*-ing*) or it is an infinitive with *to*.

2 These verbs are followed by a gerund: *imagine, feel like, suggest, practise, miss, can't stand, enjoy, detest,* and *don't mind*.

   I **enjoy cooking** but I **can't stand washing** the dishes.

3 These verbs are followed by an infinitive with *to*: *decide, refuse, hope, promise, ask, expect, afford, offer* and *choose*.

   I can't **afford to buy** a new smart phone.

4 These verbs can be followed by either form with no difference in meaning: *begin, start, continue*.

   We **started walking / to walk** towards the town.
   It **continued raining / to rain** until late afternoon.

Verbs + gerund and *to* + infinitive with different meanings

The verbs *remember, try, stop, regret, forget* can be followed by either form (gerund or infinitive) but with a difference in meaning. The difference relates to time: which action came first (1) and which came second (2). In general, verb + gerund looks back, and verb + infinitive looks forward.

Remember

I **remember going** there last year. (I went last year (1) and some time later, I remembered (2))
I **remembered to go** to the supermarket. (First I remembered (1) and then I went (2))

Forget

I'll never **forget meeting** you. (First I met you (1) and now I won't forget (2))
Don't **forget to meet** me at the cinema. (First don't forget (1) and then meet me at the cinema (2))

Stop

We **stopped eating** and left the café. (First we ate (1) and then we stopped (2))
We **stopped to eat** our sandwiches. (First we stopped (1) and then we ate (2))

Try

I **tried taking** the medicine but I still felt ill. (I felt ill. I took the medicine. After the medicine, I didn't feel better.)
I **tried to take** the medicine but I couldn't swallow it. (= I wanted to take the medicine, but I was unsuccessful.)

Regret

I really **regret telling** him what happened. (First I told him what happened (1) I am sorry that I told him (2))
I **regret to tell** you that you failed the exam. (You failed (1) and I'm sorry to have to tell you this (2))

UNIT 2

Relative clauses (review)

1 A defining relative clause identifies the thing, person, place or possession that we are talking about. We do not use a comma in these clauses.

   The woman **who** gives the lectures is very intelligent.
   (= There is only one woman who gives the lectures.)
   The city **where** I grew up is a great place. (= I am talking about the only city where I grew up.)

2 A non-defining relative clause gives additional information about the thing, person, place or possession we are talking about. This information is between commas.

   The woman, **who** gives the lectures, is very intelligent.
   (= I am talking about an intelligent woman and adding the non-essential information that she gives lectures.)
   The city, **where** I grew up, is a great place. (= I am talking about a city that's a great place, and adding that it is where I grew up.)

which to refer to a whole clause

When we want to refer back to a clause or an idea, we use the relative pronoun *which* (not *that* or *what*)

He had to go out and find a job, **which** wasn't easy.
This phone is very good, **which** is why it's so popular.

Omitting relative pronouns and reduced relative clauses

1 When the relative pronouns *that / which / who* are the object of the following clause, they can be omitted. They can't be omitted when they are the subject of the following clause.

   He's the man (**that**) I told you about.
   He's the boy **who** sold me this watch.

2. When the relative pronoun is followed by the verb *be*, we can leave out both the relative pronoun and the verb *be*. This is called a 'reduced relative clause'.

Their house, (which was) built only last year, was completely destroyed by the tornado.
The people (who are) running the company are not doing their job properly.

UNIT 3
Quantifiers

1. Quantifiers are words that we use to say how many or how much of a noun. Frequent quantifiers are:

   none, hardly any, a few / a little, (not) many / much, some, several, most, a lot / lots, loads, all

2. The quantifiers *a few / (not) many / several* are only used with countable nouns. The quantifiers *a little / (not) much* are only used with uncountable nouns.

   *I've been to **a few / many / several** rock **concerts**.*
   *They took **a little food** on the trip.*
   *They didn't take **much food** on the trip.*

3. Some quantifiers always need the word *of* before the noun or pronoun they refer to:

   ***None of** the books were cheap.*
   ***A lot of** people think that way.*

4. All the quantifiers need the word *of* when they are followed by a pronoun:

   *Hardly any films are made here, and **hardly any of them** are good.*
   *There is some food in the fridge, but **some of it** is quite old.*

5. The word *none (of)* is grammatically singular but many people use a plural verb after it.

   *I've got lots of friends, but **none of** them **are** musicians.*

so and *such* (review)

1. We use the words *so* and *such* to emphasise what we are saying:

   *This food is **so** delicious!*   *She's **such** a good writer.*

2. We use *so* + adjective. We use *such* (+ adjective) + noun (or pronoun).

   *The weather's **so** good.*   *It's **such** a wonderful day.*

3. We can follow these phrases with a *that* clause, to show consequences.

   *The weather was so good **that** we went for a walk.*
   *It was such good weather **that** we went for a walk.*

do and *did* for emphasis

We can use the auxiliary verb *do / does* (or *did* in the past) to emphasise the verb.

*I **did like** the food! I just wasn't very hungry.*
*We didn't have time to go to the museum, but we **did go** to the park.*

UNIT 4
be / get used to (doing) vs. *used to (do)*

1. When we want to talk about something being normal or familiar, we can use the expression *be used to*.

   *It's cold where I live, so **I'm used to wearing** a lot of warm clothes.*

2. We use *get used to* to refer to the process of something becoming normal or familiar.

   *It took him a while to **get used to eating** dinner early.*

3. These expressions are followed by a noun or the gerund (-ing) form of a verb.

   *I'm not really **used to** spicy **food**.*
   *They've **got used to living** in a small apartment.*

4. These expressions are not the same as *used to*, which refers to past habits or states which are no longer true and is followed by an infinitive without *to*.

   *I **used to love** their music, but now I never listen to it.*

Adverbs and adverbial phrases

Adverbs qualify verbs. They can qualify verbs in different ways, for example:

Adverbs of manner (*how*)   He walked **quickly**.
Adverbs of time (*when*)   We got there **late**.
Adverbs of place (*where*)   Sign **here**, please.
Adverbs of probability   You **probably** think I'm crazy!
Adverbs of opinion   It's **surprisingly** quiet in here.

We can also use adverbial phrases to describe a verb and to say how an action is/was performed.

One structure for adverbial phrases is *with* + noun.

*When I told her, she reacted **with surprise**.*

Another structure for adverbial phrases is *in a(n)* + adjective + *way*.

*Our teacher explains things **in a fun way**.*

Adverbial phrases are often used when an adjective (e.g. *friendly, difficult, interesting, fun*) has no adverb form.

IRREGULAR VERBS

Base form	Past simple	Past participle
be	was / were	been
bear	bore	borne
beat	beat	beaten
become	became	become
begin	began	begun
bend	bent	bent
bet	bet	bet
bite	bit	bitten
blow	blew	blown
break	broke	broken
breed	bred	bred
bring	brought	brought
broadcast	broadcast	broadcast
build	built	built
burn	burned / burnt	burned / burnt
buy	bought	bought
can	could	–
catch	caught	caught
choose	chose	chosen
come	came	come
cost	cost	cost
cut	cut	cut
deal	dealt	dealt
dive	dived	dived
do	did	done
draw	drew	drawn
dream	dreamed / dreamt	dreamed / dreamt
drink	drank	drunk
drive	drove	driven
eat	ate	eaten
fall	fell	fallen
feed	fed	fed
feel	felt	felt
fight	fought	fought
find	found	found
flee	fled	fled
fly	flew	flown
forbid	forbade	forbidden
forget	forgot	forgotten
forgive	forgave	forgiven
freeze	froze	frozen
get	got	got
give	gave	given
go	went	gone
grow	grew	grown
hang	hung	hung
have	had	had
hear	heard	heard
hide	hid	hidden
hit	hit	hit
hold	held	held
hurt	hurt	hurt
keep	kept	kept
know	knew	known
lay	laid	laid
lead	led	led
learn	learned / learnt	learned / learnt
leave	left	left

Base form	Past simple	Past participle
lend	lent	lent
let	let	let
lie	lay	lain
light	lit	lit
lose	lost	lost
make	made	made
mean	meant	meant
meet	met	met
misunderstand	misunderstood	misunderstood
overcome	overcame	overcome
pay	paid	paid
put	put	put
quit	quit	quit
read /riːd/	read /red/	read /red/
ride	rode	ridden
ring	rang	rung
rise	rose	risen
run	ran	run
say	said	said
see	saw	seen
seek	sought	sought
sell	sold	sold
send	sent	sent
set	set	set
shake	shook	shaken
shine	shone	shone
shoot	shot	shot
show	showed	shown
shut	shut	shut
sing	sang	sung
sink	sank	sunk
sit	sat	sat
sleep	slept	slept
speak	spoke	spoken
speed	sped	sped
spend	spent	spent
spill	spilled / spilt	spilled / spilt
split	split	split
spread	spread	spread
stand	stood	stood
steal	stole	stolen
stick	stuck	stuck
strike	struck	struck
swear	swore	sworn
sweep	swept	swept
swim	swam	swum
swing	swung	swung
take	took	taken
teach	taught	taught
tear	tore	torn
tell	told	told
think	thought	thought
throw	threw	thrown
understand	understood	understood
wake	woke	woken
wear	wore	worn
win	won	won
write	wrote	written

Acknowledgements

The authors and publishers acknowledge the following sources of copyright material and are grateful for the permissions granted. While every effort has been made, it has not always been possible to identify the sources of all the material used, or to trace all copyright holders. If any omissions are brought to our notice, we will be happy to include the appropriate acknowledgements on reprinting and in the next update to the digital edition, as applicable.

National Geographic Creative for the text on p. 14 adapted from 'Instants: Dispatches from the Dawn Wall' by Mallory Benedict & 'Duo Completes First Free Climb of Yosemite's Dawn Wall, Making History' by Andrew Bisharat. Copyright © 2015 National Geographic Creative. Reproduced with permission;

Eurosport for the text on p. 27 adapted from 'Quick-thinking golf star saves own life after potentially fatal spider bite' by Bunker Mentality. Copyright © Eurosport. Reproduced with permission.

Corpus
Development of this publication has made use of the Cambridge English Corpus (CEC). The CEC is a computer database of contemporary spoken and written English, which currently stands at over one billion words. It includes British English, American English and other varieties of English. It also includes the Cambridge Learner Corpus, developed in collaboration with Cambridge English Language Assessment. Cambridge University Press has built up the CEC to provide evidence about language use that helps to produce better language teaching materials.

English Profile
This product is informed by the English Vocabulary Profile, built as part of English Profile, a collaborative programme designed to enhance the learning, teaching and assessment of English worldwide. Its main funding partners are Cambridge University Press and Cambridge English Language Assessment and its aim is to create a 'profile' for English linked to the Common European Framework of Reference for Languages (CEF). English Profile outcomes, such as the English Vocabulary Profile, will provide detailed information about the language that learners can be expected to demonstrate at each CEF level, offering a clear benchmark for learners' proficiency. For more information, please visit www.englishprofile.org

Cambridge Dictionaries
Cambridge dictionaries are the world's most widely used dictionaries for learners of English. The dictionaries are available in print and online at dictionary.cambridge.org. Copyright © Cambridge University Press, reproduced with permission.

The publishers are grateful to the following for permission to reproduce copyright photographs and material:

T = Top, B = Below, L = Left, R = Right, C = Centre, B/G = Background

p. 6 (TL): ©lithian/Shutterstock; p. 6 (TR): ©Chris Whitehead/Cultura/Getty Images; p. 6 (CL): ©dogist/Shutterstock; p. 6 (CR): ©Anneka/Shutterstock; p. 6 (BL): ©Robert Hoetink/Alamy Stock Photo; p. 6 (BR): ©Jon Feigersh/Blend Images/Getty Images; p. 10: ©Jennika Argent/Moment Open/Getty Images; p. 12: ©Tracy Whiteside/Shutterstock; p. 14: ©Corey Rich/Aurora/Getty Images; p. 15: ©Kevin Foy/Alamy Stock Photo; p. 22: ©wjarek/Shutterstock; p. 23: ©mffoto/Shutterstock; p. 24: ©Andrea Willmore/Shutterstock; p. 25: ©Hero Images/Getty Images; p. 26: ©Tuul and Bruno Morandi/The Image Bank/Getty Images; p. 27 (L): ©Paul Mason/Shutterstock; p. 27 (R): ©Don Farrall/DigitalVision/Getty Images; p. 31 (a): ©Robyn Mackenzie/Shutterstock; p. 31 (b): ©OZaiachin/Shutterstock; p. 31 (c): ©nito/Shutterstock; p. 31 (d): ©Andrey_Kuzmin/Shutterstock; p. 31 (e): ©kedrov/Shutterstock; p. 31 (f): ©homydesign/Shutterstock; p. 31 (g): ©Sibrikov Valery/Shutterstock; p. 31 (h): ©BJI/Blue Jean Images/Getty Images; p. 31 (i): ©Brooke Becker/Shutterstock; p. 33: ©Tania Kolinko/Shutterstock; p. 35 (T): ©Goodluz/Shutterstock; p. 35 (B): ©michaeljung/Shutterstock; p. 36: ©Cultura RM/Craig Easton/Getty Images; p. 40: ©Fred Stein Archive/Archive Photos/Getty Images; p. 44: ©Golden Pixels LLC/Alamy Stock Photo.

Cover photographs by: (TL): ©Stephen Moore/Digital Vision Vectors/Getty Images; (BL): ©Pete Starman/Stone/Getty Images; (C): ©imagedb.com/Shutterstock; (TR): ©Stephen Moore/Digital Vision Vectors/Getty Images; (BR): ©Kimberley Coole/Lonely Planet Images/Getty Images.

The publishers are grateful to the following illustrators:
David Semple 29, 42
Julian Mosedale 5, 34

The publishers are grateful to the following contributors:
Blooberry: text design and layouts; Hilary Fletcher: picture research; Leon Chambers: audio recordings; Karen Elliott: Pronunciation sections; Rebecca Raynes: Get it right! exercises